P9-CNB-475

ADVANCE PRAISE FOR *BECOMING EVE*

"A powerful, heartfelt account of the often-fraught journey toward one's true self. In sharing her story, Abby Chava Stein lights the path for all of us who are embarking on journeys of our own."

—Tova Mirvis, bestselling author of *The Book of Separation*

"A beautiful, haunting story of self-discovery. Stein's longing for truth, acceptance, and love will echo in the heart of every reader."

—Leah Vincent, author of *Cut Me Loose:
Sin and Salvation After My Ultra-Orthodox Girlhood*

"With humor and grace—and impressive erudition of Jewish mysticism—Abby Stein grants us entry into a singular, otherworldly capsule: the byzantine world of Hasidic 'royal' families and the Sisyphean pursuit of living an authentic life within it."

—Shulem Deen, author of *All Who Go Do Not Return*, winner of the Prix Médicis and the National Jewish Book Award

"Abby Chava Stein is a compelling storyteller who shows us how to follow the voice within—even when everyone and everything around us is telling us not to."

—Rabbi Danya Ruttenberg, author of *Surprised by God*
and *Nurture the Wow*

"Abby Stein's soul-searching memoir grabbed me at the epigraph and never let me go. While religion is certainly a central element in the story, *Becoming Eve* is just as importantly about a different sense of faith: a belief in life's transformative potential to culminate in joy."

—Susan Stryker, professor of gender and women's studies, Emmy Award–winning filmmaker, and author of *Transgender History: The Roots of Today's Revolution*

"A vivid journey through Abby Stein's formative years in the Ultra-Orthodox Hasidic Jewish community as she struggles to find a more inclusive expression of her faith and learns to embrace her identity as a woman of trans experience."

—Sarah Valentine, author of *When I Was White*

BECOMING EVE

BECOMING EVE

My Journey from
Ultra-Orthodox Rabbi to
Transgender Woman

ABBY STEIN

SEAL PRESS

NEW YORK

Copyright © 2019 by Abby Stein
Cover design by Ann Kirchner
Cover image © Tawni Bannister
Cover copyright © 2019 Hachette Book Group, Inc.

Hachette Book Group supports the right to free expression and the value of copyright. The purpose of copyright is to encourage writers and artists to produce the creative works that enrich our culture.

The scanning, uploading, and distribution of this book without permission is a theft of the author's intellectual property. If you would like permission to use material from the book (other than for review purposes), please contact permissions@hbgusa.com. Thank you for your support of the author's rights.

Seal Press
Hachette Book Group
1290 Avenue of the Americas, New York, NY 10104
sealpress.com @sealpress

Printed in the United States of America

First Edition: November 2019

Published by Seal Press, an imprint of Perseus Books, LLC, a subsidiary of Hachette Book Group, Inc. The Seal Press name and logo is a trademark of the Hachette Book Group.

The Hachette Speakers Bureau provides a wide range of authors for speaking events. To find out more, go to www.hachettespeakersbureau.com or call (866) 376-6591.

The publisher is not responsible for websites (or their content) that are not owned by the publisher.

Print book interior design by Trish Wilkinson.

Library of Congress Cataloging-in-Publication Data
Names: Stein, Abby, 1991– author.
Title: Becoming Eve: my journey from ultra-Orthodox rabbi to transgender
    woman / Abby Stein.
Description: First edition. | New York: Seal Press, [2019]
Identifiers: LCCN 2019016332 (print) | LCCN 2019019987 (ebook) | ISBN
    9781580059176 (ebook) | ISBN 9781580059169 (hardcover) | ISBN
    9781580059176 (ebk.)
Subjects: LCSH: Stein, Abby, 1991– | Jewish transgender people—United States—
    Biography. | Transgender women—United States—Biography. | Hasidim—
    New York (State)—New York—Biography.
Classification: LCC BM729.T65 (ebook) | LCC BM729.T65 S74 2019 (print) |
    DDC 296.8/332092 [B]—dc23
LC record available at https://lccn.loc.gov/2019016332

ISBNs: 978-1-58005-916-9 (hardcover); 978-1-58005-917-6 (ebook)

LSC-C

10 9 8 7 6 5 4 3 2 1

To my dear son, the love of my life,
Duvid'l, to long years
Mighty waters cannot quench love; rivers cannot sweep it away.
(Song of Songs, 8:7)
Forever and Ever

לבני אהובי, מחמד לבבי
דוד שיחי׳
מַיִם רַבִּים לֹא יוּכְלוּ לְכַבּוֹת אֶת הָאַהֲבָה, וּנְהָרוֹת לֹא יִשְׁטְפוּהָ:
(שיר השירים, ח:ז)

Let me fall if I must fall. The one I will become will catch me.

—Baal Shem Tov

CONTENTS

AUTHOR'S NOTE

MY COMING-OF-AGE STORY is based on two main sources: my own memories and the stories I have been told, mostly by my parents, grandparents, and siblings. As expected from any retelling that is based on memory, especially from the years when one is a child, small inaccuracies are inevitable. I did my best to write my memories authentically and truthfully, at times consulting notes from when I was young and fact-checking with relatives who still speak to me. I was not able to speak with my parents.

In many places, I have changed the names and identifying information of the people I have written about in my story to protect their privacy.

Almost all of the dialogue in this book was originally spoken in Yiddish. When translating from any language, it is difficult to avoid slight mistranslations, and this is especially true when translating from Hasidic Yiddish, a language and dialect that has no formal method of exact translation. I did my best to recapture the words and the intentions as they were originally expressed.

INTRODUCTION

BIRTH OF AN EMPIRE

MY GRANDFATHER WAS telling me a story.

"Once, when I visited our uncle and I told him of my father-in-law, his family, and our lineage, *Der Feter* said in awe: 'Your children are among the most exalted in the world.'"

I tried not to look bored.

"You see," Zeide explained, "our family is directly descended from the Baal Shem Tov, the founder of Hasidism, and from the holiest leaders in all of Jewish history."

Whenever Zeide Stein, my paternal grandfather, spoke of *Der Feter*, I could hear the pride and respect in his voice. *Feter* is Yiddish for *uncle*, and his uncle was Rabbi Yaakov Yosef Twersky, the rebbe of the Skv'er Hasidic community, and one of the supreme leaders of Hasidic Judaism after the Holocaust. For a few years, when he was young, Zeide even lived in the Skver'a Rebbe's house so he could attend a nearby elementary school.

I had heard the vague outline of this story before and wondered where Zeide was going with all of this.

"So what?" I asked Zeide. "So our ancestors were big leaders, and holy people. What does that have to do with us?"

"Well," Zeide said, stroking his beard, "due to their holiness, their closeness to God and to the inner workings of the divine world, they secured higher souls for their children, grandchildren, and descendants for generations to come."

"Zeide, you make it seem as though we are like a medieval European regal family, when people believed that God chose the king. It's not like we're royalty," I said.

"No, no, that is exactly what we are!" Zeide interrupted. "That is exactly what I am telling you! Being direct descendants of the Holy Baal Shem Tov means that we are like princes!"

I rolled my eyes and gave Zeide a look that said *Yeah, right*. He smiled.

"Our sages have said that if the Baal Shem Tov had lived in biblical times, he would have been a patriarch. He would have been a Moses, and we would have counted him among Abraham, Isaac, and Jacob! Imagine his power! And now imagine how holy the souls of his descendants are."

What the story about *Der Feter* meant was that this illustrious lineage came down to us from multiple sources. It was not just Zeide's mother, and his uncle, who descended from the Baal Shem Tov. Zeide's father-in-law—the father of Bobbe Stein, my grandmother—had a significant lineage in Judaism as well. The complexities of my ancestry were as confounding as they were supposedly impressive.

I didn't believe most of what Zeide said about our regal stature, but by then I was fifteen years old and questioning everything I was told about religion. Besides, learning that I was somehow holier than others, which in turn meant I had to *act* holier, was not something I was interested in doing.

But I also knew that among the one million or so Hasidic people in the Ultra-Orthodox Hasidic Jewish world, it was considered a reality.

GEOGRAPHICALLY, I WAS born and raised in New York City. Culturally, I was raised in an eighteenth-century Eastern European enclave in the heart of its capital, the Ultra-Orthodox Hasidic Jewish community in Williamsburg, Brooklyn.

I grew up in New York, but I did not speak English, visit museums or the theater, or wear jeans. Popular culture, from television to newspapers to the Internet, was shunned; Britney Spears and the Beatles were not only forbidden but didn't even exist for me. I hadn't heard of *Friends* or *Seinfeld*, or many major historical events, from Woodstock to the Stonewall Riots— they were spurned topics, and we were kept from ever learning about them.

After Nazi Germany invaded Poland, the Hasidic community was all but decimated, and a few thousand families came as refugees to the United States. In New York, several Hasidic rebbes settled in Brooklyn with a hard task in front of them: rebuilding the Hasidic community from scratch. Undaunted, they set out to re-create Eastern European Hasidic shtetel life.

For the first time, the majority of Hasidic Jews were no longer living in countries where Jews were oppressed—at least, not politically. Until World War I, about half of Hasidic Jews lived in Czarist Russia, where they were confined to the infamous, poverty-ridden Pale of Settlement, which was Catherine the Great's attempt to segregate the Jews from the rest of the Russian population. Others were living under the Austro-Hungarian Empire, where they had more freedom, but the government still exercised control over their affairs. In New York, for the first time in its two hundred years of existence, the Hasidic community was living in a country that had formal separation between church and state, and where the government rarely—at least, by law—took an interest in religious communities. Not only were Jews no longer treated as outcasts, but they were reaching a new peak of influence, integration, and assimilation in the American melting pot.

But the "outside world" posed a threat, and Orthodox Jews found themselves as a tiny minority among the predominantly secular Jewish American community. So the Hasidic community added new guardrails to its own culture. In addition to creating a lifestyle that resembled life in Europe as much as possible—the food they ate, the clothing they wore, the language they spoke—the Hasidim in America developed new concepts that now came into play. While most Hungarian Jews from my grandparents' generation spoke fluent Hungarian in addition to Yiddish, their children and grandchildren were taught minimal English. And while in Europe the majority of Hasidic boys worked, mostly among non-Jews, in America all the boys would study until they got married, and most continued to study for a few years after that. The community also created an internal economy, with its own clothing, shops, brands, schools, charities, and every other organization it needed to lead an independent, homogeneous lifestyle with as little outside influence as possible.

It was in this secluded realm that my family lived a royal existence. Both of my parents descend from rabbinic dynasties—that is, the royal families of Hasidism, which have been leading the community like monarchies for the past two hundred years. My father is the tenth generation of the Baal Shem Tov, the founder of the movement—similar to a Morman being a descendant of Joseph Smith, the founder and leader of Mormonism.

I was my parents' first "boy," following my five older sisters. I was told for as long as I can remember that my father was desperate for a son, someone to take over his future synagogue—the opening of which I would one day have to witness from a distance. And I almost lived up to his dreams for me. I devoted myself to religion, and with it to family history, Hasidic theology, and family customs. I was a strong defender of our royal lineage.

Still, my piety was, in part, an overcompensation for what I recognized back then as an "evil thought" that defined my interior life: *I am a girl.*

I don't remember a day in my conscious life that I could have escaped this fact, but I tried hard. In a community that is so sheltered that it doesn't even fight or hate the LGBTQ+ community but simply ignores it, I had no idea there was anyone else like me.

Without the Internet, without English, I had no name for what I felt.

WHEN I THINK about the Baal Shem Tov, there is a particular story, one that I heard many times growing up, that comes to mind.

In a small house at the edge of the village of Okopy, in the Kingdom of Poland (modern Ukraine), the old Reb Eliezer was saying his last goodbyes to his only son, who was born to him in old age. According to Hasidic tales, Reb Eliezer was one hundred years old when the child was born, just like the biblical

Abraham when his son Isaac was born. Reb Eliezer named his only child Yisroel, and he was called Srulik'l, an affectionate Yiddish nickname. His wife passed away when Srulik'l was a baby, and Reb Eliezer would not live much longer. Srulik'l was about to become a five-year-old orphan.

"Srulik'l," the old Reb Eliezer told his only child on his death-bed, "in life, fear no one but the Divine. Love every Jew with all your heart and soul, no matter who he is."

That message of love, unconditional for everybody, regardless of who they are, followed Srulik'l for his entire life, and it became a founding principle of his teachings. The tales surrounding Srulik'l's childhood are vast, and they resemble the glorified tales that many religious movements tell about their sacred founders. There are tales of him wandering over the mountains and walking in the air. There is a widely held belief that the biblical prophet Ahijah the Shilonite came to teach him—not in his dreams, but while he was awake. There is even a letter, one that is historically authentic, from the Baal Shem Tov in which he writes of it.

It is hard to know which of these stories are accurate, fully or partially, and which are the results of hundreds of years of sanctification.

One detail of his life is surely historical: Srulik'l came into adulthood and soon launched a movement that changed the face of Judaism forever. The name Rabbi Israel Ben Eliezer, the "Baal Shem Tov"—Master of the Good Name—is revered by many. Even the twentieth-century Jewish philosopher Martin Buber said, "The Hasidic teaching is the proclamation of rebirth. No renewal of Judaism is possible that does not bear in itself the elements of Hasidism."

Although the Baal Shem Tov kept a relatively intimate group of students and followers, peaking at most to a few hundred, his students spread the message of love, spirituality, and the value of every individual person, regardless of wealth or status. With it came a dissemination of song and joy as well as populist messages that spread across Eastern and Central Europe and into Ottoman Palestine and Jerusalem. Within a hundred years, by the middle of the nineteenth century, the majority of religious Jews in Poland and Ukraine—millions of people—were at least nominally Hasidic.

After the Baal Shem Tov died in 1760, the leadership split up, and it slowly became centralized in the hands of families in which the rebbes—Hasidic Supreme Leaders—founded dynasties. Leadership then passed from father to son. Many of those dynasties still exist, and collectively they have a following of hundreds of thousands of Hasidic Jews.

Governance of the dynasties remained in the family, and Hasidic dynasties married among themselves. The children of the Baal Shem Tov married members of other dynasties, and marrying a grandchild of the Baal Shem Tov has been considered an honor for generations.

The Baal Shem Tov himself had just one son, Rabbi Tzvi Hassid of Pinsk, and from there he begat a long line of grandchildren who carried on his legacy:

Rabbi Tzvi Hassid of Pinsk had a son, Rabbi Aaron.

Rabbi Aaron also had a son, Rabbi Hersh of Skver.

Rabbi Hersh of Skver had a daughter, Sima, who married Rabbi Yitzchak Twersky, a scion of the Twersky dynasty and founder of the Skver Hasidic sect.

Sima and Rabbi Twersky's son, Rebbe Duvid of Skver, had a son, Rebbe Shlomo.

Rebbe Shlomo had a son, Rebbe Eluzer, who escaped the Bolshevik revolution and settled in Fălticeni, an industrial city in the historical Moldova region of Romania.

Rebbe Eluzer's oldest daughter, Sarah, is my great-grandmother, and the only great-grandparent who was still alive when I was born and whom I can clearly remember.

Sarah's oldest son is my grandfather, Zeide Stein, who was born in the winter of 1941 in Fălticeni.

Zeide and my grandmother had my father in 1965.

So when Zeide talked about the greatness of Hasidic dynasties, it was indeed very personal, and he impressed upon me the profundity of my own lineage: I myself share a direct ancestor with almost every Hasidic leader today.

IN THE FALL of 1982, when my father was seventeen years old, a matchmaker proposed a marriage for him with a girl from Williamsburg, Brooklyn, Chaya Sheindel Meisels. The match was promising. The young couple both came from rabbinic families, and they shared a primary goal: raise a big, devoted, rabbinic Hasidic family, in which all of their children would follow the path of Hasidic Judaism.

My parents met once and became engaged. The wedding was set for nine months later, December 1983.

"The wedding was the talk of the town," my father recalled years later. "It was attended by the biggest rebbes of the day!"

And so, a new family started. A Hasidic family, a royal rabbinic family, and a family that was destined to create rabbis, teachers, and leaders in the Hasidic world.

And me.

I was groomed from birth to follow the life-cycle path of the Hasidic tradition. There was my birth and my *bris*, or circumcision, and then my *upshern*, first haircut—and first physical distinction as a boy—at age three. My Bar Mitzvah, or entrance to adulthood, took place at age thirteen, and I became engaged to a young bride at eighteen. I got married, finished my rabbinical studies, and received the first part of my rabbinical degree following intense oral exams.

Then, in January 2012, when I was twenty, my son was born. Having a child of my own, I saw in a new light how much we gender babies before they are even born—especially within the Hasidic community—and this made it even harder for me to come to terms with my own identity. I started looking more deeply for answers about gender and faith, questioning both, along with everything else I was taught growing up.

It became more and more difficult for me to stay in the community, to stay religious, and to continue life looking like a man. The Hasidic community is—as far as my research has shown—the most gender-segregated society in the United States, and gender roles are deeply engrained in that lifestyle. Leaving would eventually become inevitable.

But leaving the community, let alone my assigned gender, was also considered deplorable.

My story includes two interwoven transitions: coming out of Ultra-Orthodoxy, and coming out as a trans woman. The stories we read of both experiences tend to suffer from problems in the public sphere, problems that are marked by overt polarization, lack of nuance, and the romanticizing of a mysterious religious sect. Several books have been written about the

Hasidic community, both by people who have lived it and left and by outsiders looking in, and most either glorify the lifestyle or demonize it. Trans representation tends to follow a similar path: there is overt sexualization and the casting of transness as mental illness, or idealized representations that focus on victimhood—though, thankfully, that's starting to change.

I am unaware of another memoir that combines both experiences. My hope is to share all of this with you: the beautiful parts of my childhood—the feelings of safety, belonging, and love that growing up in a religious, even cultish, community can offer—hand in hand with the trauma of discomfort with my body and gender in a gender-segregated society. It was a childhood that helped me to figure out who I am.

My story is my own, but it is also something greater. It is a story about arranged marriages in New York City, about a family of thirteen siblings and more than thirty aunts and uncles, of a family tree with branches as twisted as medieval European royalty. It is a portrait of life in a gender-segregated society nestled within one of the world's most progressive metropolises.

It is also a simple story of a girl coming of age.

I hope in these pages you will find a portrait of a life that every human being can relate to: the vulnerability and the glory, the frustrations and the revelations, the shedding of one identity and growing into another. No agenda, just my story.

1

BIRTH OF A CHILD

MY PARENTS WERE married in December 1983, and their marriage was soon fruitful. Just ten months after their wedding, my oldest sister, Roiza Hannah Zissel, was born. Eleven months later, my sister Ruchela was born, followed by my closest sister growing up, Esther Gitti, sixteen months after that. Faigy followed in 1988, and my fifth sister, my favorite rival growing up, Hindy, came in the summer of 1990.

In six years, the two became a family of seven, with five children, all girls.

"Everyone pities your father, poor man, he only has girls, and five of them at that!" my mother would joke.

For my father, having only girls was not a source of amusement. In the Hasidic community, having a son is what every new father dreams of and hopes for. *A son.* The traditional festivities for a newborn boy are especially grand, and a special ceremony is held thirty days after the birth of the firstborn son, when five silver coins are given to a community member who is part of the priestly family to "redeem" the child, an ancient biblical tradition. Joyous celebrating follows, with food and song. There is no similar celebration for a firstborn daughter.

Every Orthodox Jew hopes to have at least one son who will one day recite the traditional mourner's prayer after his death. And in some rabbinical families—like mine—having a son means securing a continuation of the dynasty.

After five girls, my father was beginning to lose hope, and when my mother became pregnant with a sixth child, he braced himself for another daughter.

A FEW WEEKS after a *shadchan* suggested a match between my parents, and my four grandparents had agreed it was a good pairing, both sides of the family were ready to proceed with an engagement. It was a beneficial match for everyone. My father was respectably educated in Jewish texts and was said to be a God-fearing boy who was close to finishing his studies in the complicated laws pertaining to food. My mother was beautiful, intelligent, and dedicated, a preschool teacher with a gentle nature. Not only were they both descendants of prestigious royal families, but they carried their heritage with pride; they were dedicated to the family's royal existence.

Both sets of parents had also agreed to the basic needs of the couple. They would marry in Williamsburg, and my great-grandfather, a beloved rebbe, would officiate at the wedding and the Sabbath following it. They would live in Williamsburg, too. It was even decided that following the marriage, after my mother's head was shaved, as was the custom, she would cover it with a *shpitzel*, a silk head covering made of a solid material—as opposed to a lined one that looks remotely like hair—as was the Stein family custom. My father would wear *strokes*, a long silk-

and-velvet coat resembling a graduation gown, a royal rabbinic garment worn by the Meisels family on the Sabbath—or Shabbos, as we called it—as well as on holidays, at family weddings, and during other festive occasions.

All of these details were discussed and negotiated harmoniously—until the engagement became stalled over one final issue: the color of my mother's tights.

The Meisels girls wore dark beige tights with seams—the seams being an essential feature because they ensured no one would think they were seeing bare skin. In my father's family, specifically Bobbe Stein's branch, beige was not considered modest enough, as there was still too great a risk they could be perceived as bare legs. Instead, the Stein girls wore black tights, which they considered more modest.

Bobbe Stein wanted my mother to wear black tights. Bobbe Meisels wasn't happy about it. That would mean that her married daughter would be dressing in a manner implying that her own family wasn't modest enough. Bobbe Meisels wore gray tights herself, but her daughters, like most girls in our community, wore beige, with seams.

After much debate, the grandparents reached an impasse, and the outlook for the marriage was not hopeful. Both sides hoped the other would give in.

Finally, Zeide Meisels went to his older brother-in-law, my Feter Avrom Leitner, a revered community scholar and mystic, to consult with him on the matter. Feter Avrom heard the details of the conflict, pondered, and pronounced an equitable compromise: gray was just as modest as black, he told Zeide, and so, instead of wearing beige or black, she should wear gray.

One might think that would have ended the argument. But in the Hasidic community, especially in rabbinic families, community gossip carries more weight than rabbinic declaration, and in this case, the understanding on the street was still that gray tights were less modest.

Still, it was enough to get Bobbe Stein back to the negotiating table. She called Jerusalem to consult her mother, Di Spinke Bobbe, the family matriarch.

"Gray is modest enough," the Bobbe conceded. "It is not ideal, but if the engagement hinges on it, we can make it work."

And so an agreement was made. My mother would start wearing gray after the wedding, but it was not to set a precedent; her daughters, and all future daughters-in-law, would wear black.

ON OCTOBER 1, 1991—or, the way I knew it growing up, the 24th of Tishrei in the year 5752—my mother went into labor. It was the final day of the Jewish High Holy Days season, and the last day of a nine-day holiday, Simchas Torah. If any Hasidic mother could choose a day—or, to be more precise, a night—to go into labor, the night following a holiday would be last on the list. After nine days of holiday meals, nine days of not being permitted to wash clothes for a household of seven, including five children under the age of eight, the only thing she would want to do is go home and clean up the mess.

But the mess would have to wait, because in the early afternoon hours on the last day of the holiday, my mother's water broke. During the final celebration, she dropped off my five older sisters at her parents' house, and she and my father rushed to Beth Israel Medical Center, just over the Williamsburg Bridge.

Adding to the sense of alarm was my early arrival: my mother had always carried her children full-term, but this time, she went into labor three weeks before I was due.

As they rushed my mother into the delivery room, my father's desire for a boy was stronger than ever. Most men his age were already bringing their small boys to synagogue to sit beside them during prayers and recitation of the Torah. Women and girls came to synagogue, too, but they sat in the women's section, a separate, smaller area either behind a curtain or in a gallery overlooking the main prayer hall. The practice left my father essentially childless in synagogue. My parents didn't know if I was a boy or a girl—in our community, it was not the custom to ask about a baby's gender prior to birth—so all he could do was pray for a son. As is also the custom, he waited outside the delivery room as my mother gave birth, reciting psalms and hoping for the doctor to emerge at any moment and say the words he had waited so long to hear: "It's a boy!"

Five times previously, he had waited for those words, and five times previously, he had been disappointed.

But that night he got his wish. It was a boy.

A boy!

My father was jubilant, but the celebrations in the hospital were muted. My early birth had its physical consequences, and my kidneys were underdeveloped. Three blood transfusions were necessary, two of them within twenty-four hours of my birth. My parents rushed to secure blood from the community's Jewish blood bank to prevent the use of "impure" nonreligious blood, or, God forbid, non-Jewish blood. The first transfusion had to be given just hours after birth, however, and the doctors couldn't wait; they had to use the general blood bank.

Days passed and my health slowly improved, but I wasn't yet ready to leave the hospital when my mother was discharged. For the first time, after five births with no complications, my mother had to leave the hospital without a *lichtige*, a shining baby in her arms. My father came to pick her up, and they went to stay with her parents, who lived just around the corner from their apartment in Williamsburg.

My mother waited for me there, sitting in their recliner, weeping and praying.

Days passed and I was still in the neonatal intensive care unit. My mother continued to cry and to pray to God that I would soon be well enough for her to hold me in her arms, that I could come home and grow tall and be wise.

"Perhaps now is the time for you to change to black tights," her mother-in-law, Bobbe Stein, suggested. "I am sure that your sacrifice, and commitment to modesty, will ensure the baby's health."

My mother considered this and then agreed. "All right," she said. "I promise that if my baby is healthy, I will start wearing black tights."

A few days later, my parents arrived at the hospital for a visit and were greeted with good news. "After three blood transfusions, your baby's kidneys are working just fine," the doctor said. "Tomorrow you will go home with a healthy baby!"

The joy!

Immediately, Tati (my father) began to prepare for the homecoming. A date was set for the ceremonial circumcision, which would be held in Zeide Meisels' synagogue in Williamsburg. A traditional celebratory meal was held the night before, where we were joined by close family and friends, and another followed the ceremony itself.

Right away, my mother was ready to fulfill her promise and wear only black tights.

However, my mother's sisters were not happy. "We can't have one sister dressing more modestly than the rest of us," they insisted. "What does that say about us?"

Once again, Feter Avrom came to the rescue. Hearing the renewed conflict, he assuaged the whole family, saying that "gray is actually more modest than black." His reasoning remains unclear. I can only guess that gray tights were considered more modest than black ones because they are uglier, and black is more elegant. Whatever the case, my mother did not change to black.

IN THE HASIDIC community, baby boys aren't named until their circumcision, which is usually performed on the eighth day of the child's life, as the Bible commands. Because I'd been sick, my own circumcision was delayed, and so it was that twelve days after I was born, on Sunday morning, I was finally circumcised.

The entire family gathered at the synagogue, dressed in their finest holiday clothes, and Zeide Stein held me as my father gave me my name.

"And let his name be known among Israel as *Yisroel Avrom Ben Menachem Mendel*," he declared. My father had named me after his beloved grandfather, a teacher and rebbe. In our family, we simply called him *Der Zeide*. *Der Zeide* was Zeide Stein's father. He was the Stein family patriarch, the one who had replanted the family in Brooklyn after the Holocaust, which had destroyed his home and community in Vyzhnytsia in Western Ukraine.

My parents were happy—they finally had their boy. My father would soon have a son he could take to synagogue, a son to whom he could teach Torah and the family's customs. The family was finally feeling whole.

In his wildest, worst dreams, he could not have imagined that one day, twenty years after he held his "firstborn son," that child would build up the courage to tell him, "I am a woman. I always was and I always will be."

MY FATHER DID eventually have a firstborn son, but for that he would have to wait another year. My brother Hershy, his next child, was born in January 1993. As for me, that child who was mistakenly believed to be a boy, I was to live a life entirely driven by the roles and expectations of gender. Some twenty-four years would pass before that same child stood in another synagogue, one her father would never consider to be kosher, to receive her new name.

"And let her name be known among Israel, in this community and all communities, as *Avigail Chava Bat Menachem Mendel V'Chaya Sheindel,*" the rabbi announced. Abigail Chava Stein, daughter of Mendel and Shaindy Stein.

Abby.

You see, I had gone off the *derech*—off the path. To complete my self-determination, to live an authentic life, I would have to leave the community, the most egregious offense imaginable. I left Williamsburg to build a new life in Manhattan—ten miles away, but it might as well have been another continent for all its differences.

When I left the Hasidic community, Bobbe Stein turned to my mother. "You see!" she said. "You promised God that you would wear black tights if your baby was healthy, but you broke your promise. Your baby's body might be healthy, but God took his soul."

Soon after, my mother finally started wearing black tights, and she still does today.

But let's not get ahead of ourselves. A lot happened in between.

2

A DOLLHOUSE

"LOOK, MOMMY, HERSHY sees everything!" I said, gazing into my brother Hershy's strikingly wide and beautiful eyes. He was just a few months old, and I was in awe of my new sibling.

I've always said that this is my first memory, but I would be lying if I also said I clearly remember it. It is more likely a memory based on what I was told throughout my life.

Early memories are tricky.

I was just fifteen months old when Hershy was born, and I don't recall anything from his actual arrival. I am told that I stayed with my aunt Zissi, Mommy's identical twin, and that I would mix them up at times. They looked exactly the same, and their mannerisms were similar, too. It is not hard for me to imagine that I didn't know which one was caring for me.

When I was a little older, my siblings and I would fight over who had the earliest memories, which we measured by the births we remembered: the sibling that came right after us, or the one who came after that. I always insisted that I could clearly remember my brother Efroim's birth, at which time I was two and a half. But just like my memory of Hershy's beautiful eyes, now I can't tell if I actually remember Efroim's birth or I just remember remembering.

My earliest clear, precise memories, however, are terrifying.

"My tummy hurts," I told my mother one early morning in the fall of 1993.

At age two, I was diagnosed with a hernia. In Yiddish we called it a *brakh*—literally, a "disaster"—as it happens when part of an organ or tissue grows or moves outside of its proper place inside the body. My parents took me to Mount Sinai Hospital.

"Where are we going?" I asked my mother as we rode in the hospital elevator.

"We're going to have a fun ride, and then the doctor is going to make sure you feel better, *Shefele*," she said.

I was her *shefele*, or sometimes her *shefele zisse*. Literally, it means "little lamb," and in Yiddish, it is used as an expression of endearment, like sweetheart or *liebling*. I clearly remember her calling me that, though I don't remember the sharp pains that filled my midsection. It's as if my brain registered trauma but decided to block out the bad memories and remember the sweet ones.

The elevator doors opened, and we met with the doctors. They determined that while not every hernia requires surgery, due to my young age and still-developing body, it would be too dangerous to rely on any other form of treatment. I was admitted to the hospital and placed in a small bed.

Mommy and Tati were there, too.

"Try to relax, *Shefele*," Tati said.

"You will feel better soon," Mommy soothed.

How long it took for me to actually feel better I don't remember. I do remember that after my hospital visit, my mother took me to a toy store, where I was allowed to choose a toy to bring home with me.

"Mommy, look at this dollhouse, I want this one!" I exclaimed. I loved to build fantasy homes with my Legos or Clics toys or to play house with my siblings and friends. Now I had a chance to own a real dollhouse! Even better, it was pink! I loved pink.

"Nah, this is a dollhouse," my mother replied. "I think what you really want is a truck." She turned to another shelf. "Look here, look at this fire truck! It has flashers and sirens, and if you push the button at the bottom, it moves by itself!"

I considered the truck. It did look like it could be fun. And if Mommy said it was the one I would like the best, maybe she was right.

"Dollhouses are for girls," my father chipped in. "All the boys love trucks!"

I don't know exactly what happened after that. When I search my mind, everything goes blank.

I don't know if I cried in resistance.

I don't know if I tried to beg my parents to change their minds.

Heck, I'm not even sure my father was at the store when he said what he did; maybe he said it later, when we arrived home with the truck that Mommy had recommended.

I only remember wanting a dollhouse and learning that Mommy and Tati thought it was a bad idea, something about boys and girls wanting different toys, the right toys. I remember that I was told there are differences between boys and girls, and that I was on the side of the boys.

And I remember the dark place I went after that.

Did my brain already know I was a girl? I have no idea. But an alarm was triggered—in my brain and in my body—that much is sure.

The next memory I have is from later that day, or possibly a few days later. After my surgery, it was quite some time before I could walk again, and for a while I reverted to crawling. I was crawling on the dining room floor, playing with the fire truck, lights and sirens on, "driving" it under the ten-seat table. Mommy, Tati, and my sisters stood around the table, watching me play, and I felt their eyes on me. *The Stein family finally has a boy*, I imagined them thinking.

From then on, I forced myself to like cars and trucks. My young, fragile, feminine brain did what so many girls learn to do all around the world: behave according to the social norms forced upon us if we want to survive.

Oh, and pink. I steeled myself to suppress my love for pink. It wasn't a color I saw often anyway. The palette of my childhood was dominated by blacks and grays, with an occasional burst of color—a sister's nightgown, a bunch of roses at the flower stand, where some men would buy their wives flowers for Shabbos. I'd loved the color and pined for it.

Now when I saw pink, I averted my eyes.

3

A HAIRCUT

"*GIT YOM TOV!*" Bobbe Stein exclaimed as we walked into the *sukkah*.

It was the holiday of Sukkos, the seven-day Festival of Booths that follows the High Holy Days. When I was a child, Sukkos was one of my favorite holidays. It came immediately after the Days of Awe, long days spent at synagogue where parents and teachers would talk about how we must repent to God and be better people. Meals were short, sometimes skipped entirely, and the obligations of atonement weighed heavily over our neighborhood. After weeks of this, the celebratory holiday of Sukkos was a welcome change.

At home, we built our sukkah, a seasonal dwelling. On the day after Rosh Hashanah, the Jewish New Year, Tati would go down to the shed in the backyard, bring out the wood and tools, and prepare to assemble our temporary booth.

Tati wasn't really the handiest guy, but that didn't matter. He wasn't expected to be. We grew up knowing that he was a teacher of holy lessons, and that teaching teenage boys was far more important than honing his carpentry skills. We also knew we were part of an important rabbinic family, and my father was destined to be a distinguished rabbi, maybe even a rebbe—a Hasidic Supreme Leader. Still, once a year, he took out the hammers and special nails, and with a rope, we helped him drag a pile of 8 × 2 planks of wood to our porch, where he would construct three walls, using the brick wall of our house as the fourth.

Our porch was small, but in New York City terms it was nicely sized, a generous balcony that we entered from the kitchen. Once the walls were built, Mommy and my sisters would take over and decorate them. Mommy hung the most beautiful handmade *shterns*, stars shaped from glossy paper, from the bamboo mat that formed the roof for the sukkah. There were also decorations in the shape of violins and a Torah scroll, and ones resembling the Seven Fruits that blessed the Land of Israel, all hanging from the roof and on the walls of the small hut. It was beautiful.

While my mother and sisters decorated our sukkah and cooked meals for the parade of guests who would soon come to visit, my father would walk the streets of our neighborhood, shopping for the "Four Species"—the four plants mentioned in the Bible as part of the Sukkos celebration. He would purchase an *etrog*, the fruit of a citron tree; a *lulav*, a palm frond; a *hadass*, a branch of a myrtle tree; and an *aravha*, a branch of a willow tree. Once the holiday officially began, he would bring them to synagogue with him to wave in the air during a special daily ceremony adhering to the biblical instructions: "You shall take the product of hadar trees, branches of palm trees, boughs of leafy trees, and willows of the brook, and you shall rejoice before your God" (Leviticus 23:40). The etrog and lulav are shaken in all directions—north, south, east, and west, up and down—signifying the four sides of the world, the earth, and the sky. In ancient times, and to some extent today, the holiday is all about nature. The congregation praises the Divine for a successful agricultural harvest and prays for a fruitful rain in the upcoming winter.

Many Israelis I know today like to talk about how beautiful the Jewish holidays are in Jerusalem—how you can feel the holidays in the streets, a palpable feeling of joy and celebration. Well, I have been there during the holidays, and sorry for saying so, but in Williamsburg—or, as we called it, the Jerusalem of America—it was just as glorious an event, maybe even more so. In the days leading up to Sukkos, the streets of Williamsburg, and especially the main street, Lee Avenue, are packed with tables of people selling the Four Species, sukkah decorations, and pieces of wood and bamboo that can be used to create sukkah roofs. I didn't live in an eighteenth-century Eastern European shtetel, but I imagine that Williamsburg during the holidays has a similar feel.

When I was growing up in Williamsburg, all you had to do was step out into the streets and you'd feel the holiday everywhere.

Mommy would cook and bake for weeks leading up to the holiday. On Shabbos we had the exact same traditional menu every week, but on holidays, there were special dishes. In addition to the standard challah, gefilte fish, and chicken soup with special square-shaped noodles, there were special holiday chickens and elaborate kugels. My favorite holiday food, which my mother made every year for Sukkos, was *bendel fleish*, or pickled chicken, which got its name from the *bendel*, or the netted string, that was wrapped around it during the pickling.

"LOOK WHO IS here!" Zeide Stein exclaimed as I walked into the sukkah one afternoon. "It's the *upshern yingel*!"

It's the boy who is about to get a haircut.

In the Hasidic community, boys get their first haircut on the day they turn three. Until then, their hair is left to grow, and from a distance it is difficult to tell if a small child is a boy or a girl, as both have long hair. There is no specific custom, in fact, saying that girls younger than three can't cut their hair, but it is a strongly kept tradition not to take scissors to a boy's hair until his third birthday. If a Bar Mitzvah signifies a Jewish boy becoming a man, then an upshern signifies a Hasidic child becoming a boy.

Sukkos had just ended, and it was the 24th of Tishrei, 5755, my third birthday. A grand celebration had been planned for weeks; in our dining room, my father stood with both of my grandfathers, most of my sixteen uncles, and several great-uncles. It was time.

I escaped from the dining room to the bathroom and hid. I knew what was coming, and I wanted no part of it.

To be clear, an upshern is not just a haircut. Most of the head is shaved by a razor set on a triple-zero blade, and only the sidelocks, called *payos*, are kept long. Depending on their family's custom, Hasidic men grow their payos to either the chin or the shoulder. Having long payos—a custom kept today mostly by Hasidic and some Yemenite Jews, though in the past it was common among most Eastern European, Middle Eastern, and Yemenite Jews—is based on a biblical commandment that forbids men from clean shaving the sides of their heads. As a way to show one's commitment to the word of the Torah, it became customary not only to leave the payos unshaven, but to let them grow out. Over the years, the meaning of the payos evolved to symbolize one's level of piousness. In fact, the Jews of Yemen used to call them not payos (which means "corners") but by a term that meant "signs."

My father had payos, but my mother and sisters obviously did not.

I didn't want them either.

In the bathroom, my eyes filled with tears. *Why does everyone think I'm a boy?* I thought. *I am a girl, and girls have long hair.*

It was the first time I put a thought to the feeling.

I am a girl.

Tati came to get me.

"Everyone is waiting!" he said. "It's time for you to get your beautiful payos!"

"No, no, no, no!" I protested. "Don't cut my hair, I want to have long hair! Why is Hindy allowed to have long hair and not me?"

"You are a holy boy," Tati said, trying to coax me into submission. "Girls don't get to have payos, only holy boys do!"

Tati loomed over me, his eyes full of expectancy and impatience. I knew I wasn't going to win. I went with him into the dining room, still crying.

I cried all the way through, as first Tati, then Zeide Meisels, then Zeide Stein, then all the uncles, each cut off a piece of my hair, making silly jokes and laughing among themselves. Only a few women were allowed to watch, because women who are in their menstruating years were not permitted. Mommy, Bobbe Meisels, Bobbe Stein, and my sisters stood at the kitchen doorway watching. I wanted to run to them.

I blocked out the rest of the day.

AFTER THE HAIRCUT came the fun part, or so I am told. I don't remember it myself, but in the festivities that followed the shearing, I received several presents.

First, Zeide Stein gave me my first *bekishe*, a silk coat. A bekishe is usually only worn by boys after their Bar Mitzvah at age thirteen, or, in some exclusive rabbinic families, at around age nine. In my family, though, boys wear a bekishe beginning at age three. It is so rare for a child that young to wear one that there was only one shop in Williamsburg that sold it, and even then it had to be custom made. I was a three-year-old dressed in a silk gown that cost two hundred dollars. Ah, royalty.

Bobbe Stein gave me a hand-decorated washing cup of the kind used by Hasidic people to wash their hands in a ritual called a *negel vasser*—literally, "nail water." We would fill the cup with water every night and set it by the bed, and then use it to wash in the morning before climbing out of bed. If you took more than three steps in the morning before performing the ritual, we were told, demons would follow you the whole day.

"You sure you washed *negel vasser* this morning?" Mommy would ask whenever we hurt ourselves more than once in a day.

Zeide Meisels brought me a small Torah scroll as an upshern gift. It held the entire Torah, the same as the one written on parchment in the synagogue. This one was made of plain paper, and instead of being handwritten, it was printed, but it was still a holy item to be treasured.

Bobbe Meisels brought me a toy, a small trailer with two detachable pieces, just like a real eighteen-wheeler. It had a blue front and a white back, and it soon became my favorite truck. I would decorate the white part, pretending it was a school bus.

In addition to receiving presents, I handed out packets filled with snacks and candies. It is a tradition that all Hasidic boys offer sweet things at their upshern, treats that are meant to symbolize the sweetness of the Torah and the other Jewish texts they will study.

Then, after the ceremony and festivities were over, Tati, Mommy, and all four grandparents took me to *cheder*, the boys' school. According to custom, the upshern boy is covered in a *Tallis*, the big prayer shawl that married men wear, when he goes outside on his third birthday. Tradition says that on the day a boy turns three, the Other Side—a mystical reference to evil impure forces—will do whatever it can to corrupt a boy's holiness. To ensure he doesn't see anything impure, he is covered. *Impure*, in this case, is Hasidic slang for a non-Jew, and just looking at a non-Jewish person could have negative effects for the rest of a boy's life.

When we arrived at the boys' school, we went to the first-grade classroom, where my official life of learning would begin. Inside the room, I was invited to sit on the teacher's lap, and my father and zeides sat next to us. Mommy and my bobbes stood at the doorway watching as the teacher held up a laminated plate with the Hebrew alphabet on it and asked me to repeat the letters after him.

At first I resisted, but after some playful encouragement from the teacher, I joined in.

Aleph. Beis. Gimmel.

My journey of learning had begun.

A beautiful, traumatic, loving, angry, obedient, rebellious journey.

4

ACCORDING TO HIS WILL

"STOP! WHAT ARE you doing? *Bist meshuge gevorn?*" my mother screamed as she came into the bathroom. Her Yiddish meant something like, "Have you gone totally insane?"

I was in the bathtub, taking my daily bath. I was four years old, and a few months before, my mother had started allowing me to play alone in the tub, a new privilege that delighted me.

On this day, though, I wasn't playing. Instead, after my mother had finished running the water and left, I had snuck out of the tub and taken a few safety pins that my mother often kept on the vanity by the sink. I was using them to poke and prick one part of my body: my penis. I was angry at "it" for existing, and I wanted to make it feel my pain. Poking it with a pin and feeling the sharp sting somehow made me feel better.

I'd been doing it for months, but this was the first time my mother had caught me.

"Why would you do that to yourself?" my mother screamed, equal parts worry, anger, and confusion.

"Because it doesn't belong there!" I answered. "It is a mistake that it is there!"

My mother's eyes widened. "What are you talking about?" she asked, her confusion growing.

"I want to be a girl, Mommy, and *this* does not belong on me," I insisted.

Now, I have no idea how I knew that girls don't have penises. The Hasidic community never, ever talks to children about their private parts, other than being told from a young age that they are not permitted to touch themselves *down there*. How I knew there were differences between my body and my sisters', I don't know. But I knew.

I also don't know what my mother said after that. Again, the memory of what came next is blacked out for me, and whenever I try to force my memory to recall it, I feel a shiver in my whole body.

What I do know is that whatever she said or did, it put the fear of God in me. I knew I could never, ever tell anyone how I felt. And throughout my childhood, and all through my teenage years, whenever I allowed myself a moment to consider telling someone that I felt like a girl—that I *was* a girl—the same shiver would pass through me.

STILL, I DID not give up. I could not give up. I never doubted the fact that I felt like a girl; I just had to find new ways of dealing with it. Luckily, I was blessed with a wildly creative imagination. In the years that followed, I came up with the weirdest ideas of how I could become a girl.

My favorite was an elaborate vision of an almost magical place where I would be taken and trained to be a girl. I'd be delivered to this beautiful place where only girls were allowed—girls with families who mistakenly thought they were boys. I would be surrounded by only girls and women, no boys or men, and they would teach me, directly and subconsciously, how to be a girl. The only voices I would hear would be female voices, and only women's clothing—especially women's shoes—would be permitted. (This detail of the shoes does not surprise me, as I had a fixation with women's shoes when I was little. Once when I was five, I tried to wear my mother's shoes, and my delight at slipping my feet into them was only quelled when I heard my mother's sharp screams: "You can't wear those!")

After a few months at the girl-training site, I would come home a lovely girl, unrecognizable to my family and neighbors as my former "boy" self. In my fantasy, I was not just pretty but *the most beautiful girl in the world*; for having suffered through years of being forced to live like a boy, I was rewarded with an otherworldly beauty.

My vision didn't end there. Once I was home, I would finally get to play with my girl cousins and friends. I never got along with boys; it was girls' company I craved. We would trade pink Hello Kitty stationery, play and dance together, and play dress-up in gowns and petticoats.

"Look at her, she is just *adorable*," my aunts would whisper.

I spent countless nights in bed creating these complex fantasies. I conjured this particular fantasy so many times that I began to dream about it, and the boundary between dreaming while asleep and fantasizing while awake became blurred.

Then the dark thoughts would come.

I must be crazy, I would think. *There is no one else in the world who feels like I do. I am the only girl who is being raised as a boy.*

And: *Something must be very wrong with me.*

Another common fantasy, and a favorite dream, was that I'd be reborn as a girl.

In some magical way, I would end up in a mother's belly and by coming out again it would correct me. I mean, a mother's belly creates girls, right? Well, I would be reborn. Every time I heard someone was pregnant, whether it was my own mother, an aunt, a neighbor, or a total stranger, I would imagine how I would take the baby's place and come out as a girl.

In the fall of 1997, my mother became pregnant with her tenth child, my brother Baruch. It was her hardest pregnancy, and during the third trimester she had to be connected to IV fluids for most of the day. There she was, walking around with an IV pole, and we were only told that "Mommy isn't feeling so well, so she has to be connected to a special soda."

I knew she was pregnant. I was also sure that the reason why this pregnancy was so difficult was that her body had to do a lot of extra work to drag me into it and rebirth me as a girl.

Baruch was finally born on the seventh day of Hanukkah in the Hebrew year 5758—that is, December 29, 1997, by the Gregorian calendar—and we got a phone call saying that Mommy had had a baby boy. In the moment, I forgot about my own fantasy and cheered with my siblings, who were dancing on the beds from excitement. The baby might have been the tenth child in our family, but it was still exciting.

Soon after, I gave up on the crazy idea of being reborn.

Instead, I came up with a better idea.

I loved reading from a very young age. At age five, I learned to read Hebrew and Yiddish without the vowels, something most students only learn at around eight or nine years old. With this new skill, I started reading anything I could get my hands on, from the weekly Yiddish magazine *Oneg Shabbos* (*The Joy of Shabbos*) to the monthly magazines *Ma'alos* (*Ascent*) and *Der Blick* (*The View*) that I pushed Tati to subscribe to. I'd find long Yiddish novels like *Nein un Neintzig* (*Ninety-Nine*), and the crime novel *Der Risokalisher Gerongel* (*The Risky Battle*), and read them cover to cover, over and over again.

I would go to bed early so I could read without being questioned, and when my mother came in to shut out the light, I would hide what I was reading under my pillow, and then continue to read in the dark.

Then, at around age seven, I started reading newspapers.

Every week, Tati bought two Yiddish newspapers that were published by the community: the establishment *Der Yid* (*The Jew*), the oldest Hasidic newspaper published in Yiddish, which was founded in the 1940s and is still going strong, and *Di Tzeitung* (the *News Report*), a relatively independent and smaller— though, in my opinion, higher-quality—community weekly.

Every Wednesday, when *Di Tzeitung* arrived, and every Thursday, when *Der Yid* was released, my sister Esther Gitti, the other avid reader in the family, and I would fight over who got to read it first. Our parents tried to negotiate between us, but we developed a few tricks to leverage control over the pages. The most common tactic was taking the newspaper and escaping into the bathroom. There were countless times when I stood waiting outside the bathroom for Esther Gitti to come out with the paper.

These papers were full of fascinating information, and we both loved the serialized stories. But the best part was that they brought me a new strategy for becoming a girl. In the health section, I learned about an exciting concept: organ transplants.

Almost every week, I'd find at least one story of a transplant. Some told of people who were waiting for transplants; others were informational articles, describing particular transplant procedures. Some weeks, there would be a call to help a patient who was in need of a kidney or lung. I collected them all.

After two years, I had collected newspaper clippings about almost every possible transplant. There were articles about heart, kidney, lung, and liver transplants, and even stories about experimental transplants of unusual body parts, like hands and legs.

They all fueled my new plan to become a girl.

The plan was simple. One day, I would have enough articles to know how to do a full-body transplant. Then, I would go to a doctor, show the doctor my impressive collection of newspaper clippings, and the doctor would perform a full-body transplant, putting me into the body of a girl. It made perfect sense.

Until it didn't. Eventually, by the time I was around nine, I realized that a full-body transplant was impossible. Frustrated, I threw out my collection of newspaper clippings. It was time to move on. I'd have to figure out another way to finally be a girl.

I would not give up.

But what could I do?

I was always told that God can help with anything. Well, maybe it was time to turn to God. After all, I figured, since I was apparently the only girl in the world who was told I was a boy, only *Der Bashefer*, the Creator, could help me.

I wrote a prayer:

Holy Creator, I am going to sleep now, and I look like a boy.
I am begging you, when I wake up in the morning, I want

to be a girl. I know that you can do anything, and nothing is too hard for you, so please, I am a girl, why can't I look like a beautiful little girl?!

If you do that, I promise that I will be a good girl. I will dress in the most modest clothes, I will listen to everything Mommy and Tati ask, and I will keep all the commandments girls have to keep, in the best way possible.

When I get older, I will be the best wife. I will help my husband study Torah all day and all night, I will cook the best foods for him and my kids. I will have the nicest Shabbos table, and I will have as many babies as I can.

God, you have enough boys, you do not need me to be a boy. I promise, if I wake up as a girl, I will make up for it by having many boys, who will be the most studied and pious boys. I want to give birth to girls when I am older, but if you listen to me now, I am ready to make an exchange: Let me be a girl, and I will be happy to have a big family with just boys.

Oh God, help me!

I offered this prayer every night after my brothers and sisters and I said our bedtime blessings. We recited the *Shema*, "Hear O Israel, the Lord is our God, the Lord is One," and Psalm 31, "In Your hands I leave my spirit."

Then, every night for three years, I added my own silent prayer before I went to sleep. I said my special prayer with devotion, with a full concentration of heart and mind, the way I had been taught.

I finished my private ritual by reciting the traditional blessing that girls say every morning. Boys were taught to thank God each day by proclaiming, "Blessed are you, O Lord our God,

King of the Universe, who did not make me a woman." But girls said this instead, and so I did too:

Blessed are you, O Lord Our God, King of the Universe, who has made me according to His will.

Only then would I go to sleep.

5

ON THE PLAYGROUND

"**W**HY ARE YOU not in the *shpiel platz*?" my teacher asked me, tipping his head to gesture toward the playground.

"I don't enjoy the games they are playing," I replied.

I had just turned ten and was in fifth grade at the Shopron Hasidic School.

No one in the Hasidic community attended public school, heaven forbid. Public schools were frightening, dangerous places where the *goyim* went, where it was rumored that students killed their teachers on a regular basis. Instead, Hasidic children were sent to private schools that were aligned with their specific Hasidic sect.

In Williamsburg, most schools were associated with the communities of Satmar, Pupa, Viznitz, Vien, Tzhelim, Skver, and so on, all sects that were named after the Eastern European villages their progenitors came from after the war. The largest sect in Williamsburg, and therefore the largest school, was the Satmar school, with more than ten thousand students.

I didn't attend a school of my family's own sects, though; instead, I was sent to Shopron, a school that was even more religious, and that happened to be founded and led by Zeide Meisels' first cousin, Reb Hershel Meisels, the rabbi of the school. But that was not the main reason my brothers and I went there. We attended the school because Tati was a *Magid Sheir* in that yeshiva, meaning that he taught the subject of Jewish law to the tenth-grade students. As an employee, his children were granted free tuition, and with five boys attending school, that added up to a savings of around $1,000 a month. So of course that's where we went.

It also helped that the education was considered better there, with only about twenty-five students per grade. In the bigger schools, which some of the adults called a "child factory," there were easily five hundred boys per grade, and often over thirty students per class.

Shopron was aligned with the Satmar sect, but this didn't bother Tati or Mommy much, even though we were not fully Satmar. While both sides of my family originally belonged to different Hasidic sects—the Stein family had followed the Viznitz Hasidic sect since the eighteenth century, and the Meisels were Bobov Hasidim and direct descendants of the first Bobov'er Rebbe—they were both heavily influenced by Satmar after the war. As such, they felt comfortable with the principles and teachings of the Satmar rebbes.

After the war, even Zeide Meisels' father recognized that the newly formed Satmar sect was growing quickly in the United States. The Satmar practices closely resembled the vision he had of replanting Hasidic life in America. The fact that Zeide Meisels' father and the Satmar Rebbe were first cousins helped.

So, he formed a quasi-alliance with Satmar. He himself never became a Satmar Hasid, but most of his sons did. One of his sons, Feter Duvid from Montreal, Zeide Meisels' brother, even married the Second Satmar Rebbe's daughter.

Zeide Stein's father had a slightly more complicated relationship with the Satmar sect. He was a Ukrainian Jew through and through, and as far as I can tell, could never see himself as fully part of a sect that consisted of mostly Hungarians. However, just like the Meisels family, he saw the Satmar Rebbe as a powerful entity who was better kept close, so close he went. Still, *Der Zeide* never stopped being a devout Viznitz Hasid. All his customs, clothing, and songs were Viznitz. His three sons all attended Viznitz schools and yeshivas, the older two, including Zeide Stein, in Israel, and the youngest in Monsey, New York.

When the Satmar Rebbe Yoel Teitelbaum passed away in 1979, the Stein family stopped following the Satmar rebbes altogether. They maintained relationships with a few of his followers, as friends and professional colleagues, and sometimes by marriage. But their only true rebbe, the one spiritual leader that mattered, was the Viznitz'er Rebbe.

So, there I was, a mostly Viznitz child attending a school that was dominated by Satmar Hasidim. I was in the perfect position to find a new way to rebel: everyone there followed the rules of the Satmar sect, so I would follow the rules of the Viznitz. It was the perfect strategy for a girl who was attending a boys' school and wanted to rebel while still being a good student. It was perfect.

OUR EDUCATION IN elementary school was driven by an intense regimen of learning and consisted almost entirely of Judaic studies. Six days a week we read and recited Torah and Talmudic teachings. We went to school for five full days, Sunday to Thursday, and then an additional half day on Friday, when we went home at around noon to prepare for Shabbos.

I was envious of my sisters, who stayed home on Sundays.

"Why do I have to go to school on Sunday but the girls don't?" I asked my mother one day.

"Well, boys have to learn the holy Torah, so you can't waste time," she replied.

That is the mentality around education in the Hasidic community. For boys, every minute spent on anything other than Jewish studies is wasted time. For girls, the primary goal is to marry, have babies, cook, and be proficient housewives, and so their schooling is less rigid. Yes, it is important even for girls to know how to read and write Hebrew and Yiddish, and to know how to pray and how to observe holidays properly. But it is just as important that girls should know how to cook meals for their family and mend clothes. And if someone in the family must speak passable English? Well, let it be the girls who learn that, because boys have more important subjects to study.

As a result, my sisters' schools looked quite similar to secular schools. They followed the same schedule, the same five-day week, with similar vacation time. Boys' schools had a very different system.

We started first grade at around age five, instead of six as in most secular schools, to allow for more years of full education. By fourth grade, the school day is elongated to last from 8:30 a.m. to 5:00 p.m. Our schedule looked something like this:

The school bus picked us up at around 8:15 in the morning, and by around 8:30 we were in the school dining hall eating breakfast.

At around 9:15 we assembled for morning prayers, which was followed by about five minutes of reciting psalms and another fifteen minutes of studying morality. Then came the morning study period, which most days was filled with Torah study. We'd learn the text and lessons of the weekly portion of the Bible.

From 11:30 to 11:45 we had a short recess, and then we went back to class until 1:00 p.m.

At 1:00 p.m. we ate lunch, and then came the dreaded forty-five minutes of playing in the *shpiel platz*, an indoor playground.

At 2:00 p.m. we returned to the classroom, where we said the afternoon prayers. Then came the second study session of the day: Talmud, the sixth-century rabbinic text, the foundation of rabbinic Judaism.

At 4:00 we began our secular studies, either English or math.

At 5:00 we headed home.

The English we learned was minimal, as was the time devoted to it. English was taught only a few days a week, and only between the fourth and eighth grades. That was more than enough, deemed the rebbes. They also permitted us to learn some math, starting in fourth grade with simple addition and subtraction. By the end of eighth grade, the good students knew how to solve long division.

There were no classes in social studies, none in US history, no world history, no science.

By the end of eighth grade, when we stopped having any general education, I doubt there was a single student who could carry on a full conversation in English.

The last reading book we ever used, an "advanced" one in eighth grade, was a book about the US Mint. I loved that book; it had a nice green cover and some interesting pictures, and it talked about the history of currency. It was the only non-Jewish history we ever learned.

Years later, I looked up that same book to find out where it fit in with the New York Regents curriculum and public school system. It was a third-grade book.

This was fine with my parents, who weren't concerned in the least with my secular academic performance. When I took home my quarterly report card, my mother never even looked at the side that displayed my grades for the secular subjects. She only scanned the side that showed my marks for behaving well, participating in class, and being nice to other students. As long as I had straight A's there, she was happy.

Learning was easy for me, but socializing was not. As I reached fourth and fifth grades, the pool of kids I could be friends with narrowed significantly.

I was a good student. I came from not just a nice family, but a prestigious, rabbinic family. Other students loved talking with me, and I had some great stories to tell, both real and fictitious. Yet I did not have friends for two reasons.

First, I hated playing with the boys, and second, I was terrible at playing with the boys.

Playing with girls, whether they were cousins or neighbors, had long ceased to be an option for me. By the time I was six, boys and girls were not permitted to play together. This seemed to suit everyone else, but as a girl who was thought to be a boy, I was at loose ends.

Meanwhile, the kids on my block enjoyed a robust social street life. The boys rode their bikes, traded rebbe cards, and played made-up ball games using rolled-up belts as balls, as real balls were considered off-limits. The girls chatted, traded pretty stationery from their collections, and jumped rope.

We lived on one of only six blocks in the entire neighborhood in Williamsburg that had semiprivate houses. The houses were all built in rows, with alleyways, front yards, and backyards, and only one family per floor. The Brooklyn Villas, where we lived, were built in the early 1990s, and they were full of young families. Almost every family on the block had somewhere around ten kids, and with all the open spaces around, it was the perfect environment for them to play together when it was warm outside.

I was expected to play with the boys, but I hated not just boys' sports but also the way boys were when they spent time with each other. We might have lived in the most isolated and sheltered society in New York, but aggression still found its way in. Living in the most gender-segregated society in the Americas, and constantly being told that boys are better than girls, did not help either.

I'd have much preferred to be with the girls, trading colorful paper and baby dolls, playing with each other's hair, and talking about clothes. Heck, I would have even enjoyed talking about being a housewife and cooking.

Do I think this is what makes a girl? No. Yet I couldn't help my feelings.

I couldn't do any of that anyway.

Instead, I would stay home and read.

Mommy tried many times to get me to play with the other boys, and she meant well; she wanted me to have friends. She wanted me to be happy. Finally, she realized that I really was happier staying home, reading and playing on my own, and she let me be.

IN SCHOOL, IT was a different story.

During lunch hour, from third to fifth grades, there were no alternatives. Everyone was expected to be in the *shpiel platz* and participate.

Some days we played Catch the Flag, with a belt standing in as the flag. Other days we played Red Rover, though we didn't call it that—we called it "Right Over." Still, it was played the same way: two teams lined up on opposite sides, holding hands tightly. The first team would call out the name of a student on the other team, who would have to run across, crashing into the clasped hands of the chain of boys on the first team. If the student could break the chain, he went back to his team; if not, he had to join the opposing team. This process was repeated, each side taking turns.

Other popular games were *Kokolach*, which involved juggling five small rocks, and Pinocchio, a game resembling musical chairs in which you tried to step on other kids' toes.

None of these were interesting to me. Crashing into each other? Stomping on each other's feet? These were not my ideas of fun.

Reb Walter, the fourth-grade teacher, supervised us in the *shpiel platz* during lunchtime. He stood at the entrance to the play area, watching us run around and breaking up fights when they erupted, which they did a few times every day. He was responsible for dividing the teams fairly and making sure every student had a chance to play.

My aversion to joining in was not to his liking.

"Have you tried to play? I am sure there is at least one game you would enjoy," he cajoled.

"No, I don't enjoy any of these games. Unless it is just trading cards or schmoozing, I hate the games boys play!" I protested many times.

At first, he tried to force me to play. More than once he took me over to a team and told them they had to include me in their game. He meant well; he wanted to help me fit in.

When I couldn't get rid of him, I would look for ways to sneak out of the *shpiel platz*. I'd say I needed to use the bathroom, and then sneak over to the high school section of the building, where I would often find Tati taking his lunch break. Sometimes Tati would also try to encourage me to play, but most of the time he knew better. Instead, I'd sit in Tati's office and nibble at his lunch, usually a chocolate Danish, and chat about everything and anything. I was happy there.

Finally, by the middle of fifth grade, Reb Walter gave up.

"Listen, you do not have to play, but you have to be in the *shpiel platz*," he told me.

So for the next two years, I would sit in quiet corners during lunch and talk with the one or two friends I had.

IN SIXTH GRADE, I made one of my closest friends. His name was Zalmy, a shy, smart kid, what we would call nerdy today, with bright brown eyes. He was the only other student I knew who had an interest in politics. Hasidic kids rarely talk about politics, not because it is forbidden but simply because no one seems to care.

This was right after September 11, 2001, at the beginning of the invasion of Afghanistan, and Zalmy and I both learned of current events from the same heavily censored Hasidic newspapers. For reasons that I do not understand today, I liked George W. Bush, so naturally I declared myself a Republican. Zalmy was still angry from the 2000 election, when he liked Al Gore, so he declared himself a Democrat. Neither of us had any idea what it meant to be a Republican or a Democrat, beyond the vague awareness that they were two teams with different leaders.

In eighth grade, during the 2004 presidential election, we published a handwritten political newspaper in Yiddish. He was the Democratic columnist, rooting for John Kerry, and I was the Republican columnist, rooting for Bush's reelection. We both got in trouble for handing out "political" writings in class, writings that, while they were not forbidden, were also not desired, and that was the end of our journalism careers.

I didn't really mind. To me, politics was just a hobby. It filled my time so I wouldn't have to play games with other boys. Finally, later that year, I was given an alternative to playing: I was allowed to stay in the study hall to study any Jewish subject or book I wanted.

Reprieve!

I started by studying the Hebrew calendar, a hobby I still have today. The Hebrew calendar follows a complex mathematical structure based on cycles of nineteen years, during which the lunar and solar calendars even out. While it's generally thought that the Hebrew calendar is simply lunar based, it is actually a mix of both lunar and solar. The calculations are made according to many rules with complicated exceptions, such as leap months with an extra day and leap years with an extra month.

Later, I would branch out to other texts, reading and studying unconventional books. One of the books I loved was called *Seder*

Hadorot (*Book of Generations*). It is a canonized medieval-based text that recounts the history of the world according to Jewish and apocryphal traditions, from year one of creation to around the fifty-fifth century of the Hebrew calendar.

That small opening to study set me free. I was through with the brutal games of roughhousing boys. A door had opened for me, and I could now follow my own path of learning, of questioning, and of craving truth and knowledge, a craving I still have today.

6

SEEING DEMONS

I T WAS A dull and cloudy day in the eighth grade and my classmates and I were hunkered down at our desks, studying a section of the Talmud dealing with divorce—specifically, the laws
in the seventh chapter of the tractate of Gittin, a second-century
text from the Mishna, addressing a man's wish to divorce his
wife when she is possessed by a demon.

The reference to a demon is not literal; instead, it means the
wife is mentally ill. In ancient times, there was no understanding of insanity, and the only way to explain psychotic behavior
was to attribute it to a demon. Still, the Talmud devotes several
pages to the problem of demons—how they might come to possess one's body, how to get rid of them, and even how one can
see them with the naked eye, a process that involves sprinkling
the ashes of a black chicken around the bed.

My teacher read the text aloud, and my classmates nodded
their heads. No one questioned the rationality of demon posses-
sion, or of the metaphysical powers of chicken ashes.

I raised my hand.

"Yes, what is your question?" Reb Mendelovitz asked.

"Can I try this at home?" I said, with a hint of a smirk. "If I do, will I be able to see demons?"

For a moment he was quiet. Then his face rearranged itself into an expression of anger.

Then he kicked me out of the room.

"Get out!" he shouted, pointing to the door.

This was not the first time I had challenged his teachings, but it was the last straw. I left the room feeling his glare follow me.

That night, he called me to his father's synagogue to have a chat. I sat across from him, trying to avoid the stern, concerned look in his eyes.

"If you continue to ask questions like these, you will end up going off the *derech*," he said.

Off the *derech*, off the path. By questioning his teachings, I was straying from our religious laws, the worst possible offense. His lecture was a warning, one that leaders in the Hasidic community often use to instill fear in children. It was the equivalent of a parent telling a teenager, "If you continue to act up, you'll wind up in a prison cell one day."

He was right, and he didn't even know how much. Neither did I at the time.

Still, being expelled from class was usually reserved for troublemakers who physically disrupted the class order. It was the first time I had ever been sent out of the classroom, and, as far as I know, it was the only time a student had been kicked out for asking a question.

Okay, fine, the question was bordering on heresy—but still.

And yet I felt bad. I liked Reb Mendelovitz. For the most part, I enjoyed his teaching, as well as the thoughtful materials he provided for us to study. Many teachers would go a whole year without bringing worksheets or handouts to augment our studies, and if they did, the students still had no opportunity to share their own writings. Without a schoolwide student publication of any kind, that meant students never had the opportunity to share their own ideas about the subjects they were studying, or about anything else, for that matter. Reb Mendelovitz was different. He encouraged us to participate—to think, to speak, to care.

And he had been kind to me, something I needed in a school that felt otherwise distant and occasionally hostile. Once, he had given me a Student of the Month medal, praising my perfect written Hebrew and my attention to the smallest discrepancies in the subject matter. He said I had an *eisener kup*, a "steel head," an expression for a bright mind. I knew he liked me and wanted the best for me.

But this time I'd gone too far, and I'd incited his anger and his concern. I left the synagogue feeling ashamed.

"WHAT DO YOU want to do after school now?" Tati asked me.

It was a cold winter Saturday night not long after the classroom altercation over conjuring demons, and my father and I were on our way home. We had just attended a beautiful *siyum*, a religious occasion celebrating a significant learning accomplishment, such as completing the study of a sizable portion of the Talmud. I had recently had a *siyum* myself; in three years, I had finished studying the entire part of the Talmud addressing the laws of the holidays. It is one-sixth of the entire Talmud, and many people, even those who study regularly, never finish it. To finish in eighth grade was a true achievement.

My own celebration had been held on a Saturday night, a few months into eighth grade. I had sat with five other students who had also completed the study at a head table, where everyone wished us mazel tov and gave us presents. We each received our own set of Talmud books, all twenty volumes, something most Hasidic people get only as a wedding gift.

As Tati and I walked down the quiet streets of Williamsburg, I thought about the afternoons I'd now have free, now that I wasn't obligated to attend a special after-school program for Talmud study. That's when Tati raised the topic of my Bar Mitzvah.

"Now that you are closer to your Bar Mitzvah, it is not the time to waste your afternoons. You are about to become a young man, and you have to take religious study and divine worship even more seriously."

He went on with his fatherly lecture, but I stopped listening, fixating on the words he had just said.

Bar Mitzvah.

Young *man*.

His words landed like a bomb, and my ears thundered with noise. As we walked through the underpass under the BQE at Wythe Avenue and Williamsburg Street East, all I could take in was the sound of the cars above me. The cracks in the sidewalk asphalt under my feet seemed as though they were going to swallow me, and my heart raced.

I was a girl being raised as a boy, and I was going to have a Bar Mitzvah.

Of course, this was not a surprise to me. Of course I was going to have a Bar Mitzvah. The date had been chosen long ago, and a venue had been booked. Tati had even ordered *Tefillin* for me to wear—a set of small black leather boxes containing scrolls of parchment that were inscribed with verses from the Torah, to be worn on my forehead and on one arm during prayer after my Bar Mitzvah.

But knowing and feeling are not the same.

Now I felt it, and it felt terrible. I felt as if Tati had just told me I had a terminal illness.

I could no longer hear his words, but I could hear his voice, and I needed it to stop. I spun around and glared at him.

"I do not want to talk about this!" I shrieked.

Tati had no idea what had befallen me. "Why are you scream-ing?" he asked. I didn't answer; I stormed ahead, silent and fum-ing all the way. When we reached our house, I ran straight to my room, climbed into my bed with all my clothes on, and cried.

My parents were bewildered. This was not my first outburst, and they were growing more and more concerned. They knew little kids had temper tantrums, and older children were prone to mood swings. My parents knew how to deal with them, just like they did with my siblings.

But my outbursts were different. They were random, explo-sive, and seemingly unexplainable.

My parents didn't understand, but I did. Waves of anger and panic swept over me whenever I connected to the idea that no one saw me as a girl, that no one saw me for me. It made me feel lost, and helpless.

As I cried under my covers, Tati and Mommy stood outside, worrying.

"Something is wrong with him," I heard Tati say. "I think he is hiding something, something existential, something big. Maybe we need to send him to a therapist." Therapists weren't common in our community, but they did exist.

I sat up on my bed, and I spoke out loud to myself: "I am not a girl. It is impossible. No one else feels like this. Something must be confusing me, making me think I am a girl when I am not."

I had said this before, enough times that sometimes I was almost able to convince myself that it was true. But it wasn't.

AT THAT TIME, I convinced myself to let go of the "crazy idea" that I was a girl, and instead I found a different reason why I was having such a strong identity struggle. I turned to the next biggest part of my identity, religion, and focused my scrutiny there. Every chance I had, I demanded answers to what eluded me.

"Who said there is really a God? Who said Judaism is the right religion? Who said Hasidic Judaism is the right way to be Jewish? Do we even have souls?"

These might sound like the kind of everyday questions many teenagers in the Western world ask at some point in their lives. Questioning is basic human nature, and for most Jews around the world, it is a strong Jewish value. Not in the Hasidic community. My questions were met with disdain and anger, and shock. Asking these questions was just not done. I didn't know of any other teenager who questioned the existence of God, the ultimate truth of Judaism as the only true path to God, the fact that we were the chosen people, or even the authority of our late sages.

For me, it was necessary. I had no faith in anything I was told; if every authority in my life told me I was a boy, and I knew I was a girl, how could I believe the rest of their claims? If they were wrong about my gender, they could be wrong about God, too.

It was around this time that something dawned on me that I had not considered before: Most people in the world are not Jewish, and most Jews are not religious.

I was astounded.

I was a child living in a city of 8.5 million people, the majority of whom were not Jewish, and I had had no idea.

There were more Jews in New York than in any other city in the world, but most of them were not Orthodox, and I had had no idea.

The irony was monumental.

The Hasidic community's ability to fashion a protective sheath around our lives was masterful. We did not just live in a bubble, we took the bubble with us wherever we went. I have aunts, uncles, and cousins on three continents, and extended family on all six inhabited continents. They all speak the same language, wear the same clothing, eat the same food, and live in the same kinds of neighborhoods. There are only the smallest of differences between Hasidic people from New York and those from London, Antwerp, Melbourne, South Africa, and São Paulo. So while no one had ever told me, exactly, that Hasidic people constituted most of the population of the world, Hasidism was all I ever knew, and so I assumed.

When it dawned on me that perhaps we were not the majority I had imagined, I asked my father if it could be true. My father confirmed my suspicions.

"Really?" I asked Tati. "The One Above created a whole world with billions of people, but only a few million are his chosen people? Everyone else is just—what? Do they have no souls? Are they just waste?"

"Yes!" he replied and quoted the Talmud: "The whole world was created for us, because of us, and we are the only people with souls, the only people that matter in the cosmic sense."

He said this with full assurance, as though he were confirming that we breathe oxygen and that rain falls from the sky.

I refused to believe him.

I refused to believe.

7

AT THE EDGE OF MANHOOD

"WHY DO YOU keep staring at your *veise zoken*?" Mommy asked. It was the day before the nine-day holiday of the Sukkos festival, and I had just put on my long white socks, worn only by adult men on Shabbos and holidays, for the first time. While wearing short pants with long white socks, eighteenth-century style, is very common in the Hasidic world, it is extremely rare for teenagers.

"I love the way they look. They're cute!" I responded.

Mommy's face contorted into a strange expression, kind of a mixed reaction between weirded out, confused, worried, and pitying.

"What do you mean, 'They're cute'?" she said. "That is a very girlish thing to say. You are about to become *bar mitzvah*, you have to act like a young man!"

"It is okay, don't worry," Tati jumped in. "It's just new to him," he soothed her. But I heard the worry in his voice, too.

What was not new to me was the regimented dress code, down to the socks I was expected to wear. The clothing requirements for Hasidic people are precise and strictly enforced, and oriented around maximizing modesty—that is, modesty based on eighteenth-century ideas of decorum and style.

For women, it requires "quiet"-colored clothes, with fully covered collarbones, ankles, and knees. Pants, of course, are not allowed. Married women must shave their hair and then cover their heads with various versions of headwear—knitted caps, sometimes, or a *shpitzel*—a partial wig with a scarf around it. Women also must wear dark, opaque tights at all times, beginning in the ninth grade. On Tati's side of the family, there were rules about girls never wearing loose hair, something Bobbe Stein was particularly impassioned about, and so my sisters always wore a pony tail, and most of our cousins always kept their hair in a braid.

On Friday nights and holidays, my mother and my married sisters wore a *shtern tichel*. This is a piece of brown material that wraps closely around the head, covering the hairline in front and falling low in the back. The base of it looks something like a swim cap, and on top of that is a royal component: a beautiful tiara, made out of pearls. While the women would sometimes grumble about the brown piece—some loving it and some hating it, no opinions fell in between—the tiara was striking and beautiful. Whenever anyone in my family walked outside with the *shtern tichel*, passersby would turn their heads. It said one thing, and it said it loudly: *I am royalty.*

In my childhood fantasies about living as a beautiful girl, the *shtern tichel* played a prominent role. For years, I dreamed of the day I would be able to wear it.

There is a far heavier focus on women's modesty in Hasidism than there is on men following the dress code, but men are hardly exempt. They are expected to dress mostly in black and white clothes, with long coats worn year-round. Black hats complete the outfit, and, for married men, fur hats, called *shtreimel*, are to be worn on Shabbos and on holidays.

As a rule, anyone who breaks the modesty rules is punished—if not literally, then socially. If a married woman leaves her home without a head covering, neighbors will raise eyebrows. Clothing too tight? Arms and legs not fully covered? Unacceptable. Men can get away with not wearing a hat every moment of the day, but wearing colored shirts or any styles that are considered "too modern" will get them into hot water.

Beyond these basic guidelines for all Hasidic people is the *rebbishe* dress code—the unique dress code for people of rabbinic descent. Every family has its own set of rules and regulations, its own prescribed combination of clothes, with no details left for variation or individuality. The shade of a piece of velvet, thickness of a belt, and shape of a hat can say volumes about which family one belongs to.

"Why do we dress differently than everyone else?" I asked Tati when I was small.

"Because we are special," he replied. "We are holy because of our ancestor, and we follow our traditions more closely. We are like princes!"

Tati was proud of our heritage, and I was, too, I suppose, though it also made me uncomfortable. Wearing boys' clothing was difficult enough; being forced to stand out at all times by the differences in my clothing was discomfiting.

"I want our boys to wear *veise zoken and a kolpik*," I remember Tati saying one Friday night at the Shabbos table. A *kolpik* was a brownish fur hat that some boys of rabbinic descent wore as teenagers—other men wore fur hats only after they married.

Mommy intervened.

"I am okay with just one of those," Mommy responded. "Both is just too much!" By too much, she meant that it would draw too much attention to us. We would be perceived as egoistic, loudly announcing that we were royalty. Tati ultimately agreed, and we wore only *veise zoken*. At the time, I didn't think much of it, but later I came to learn how right Mommy was about it being "too much"—just wearing the white socks made me conspicuous. Every time I wore them, I could feel everyone's eyes moving down to look at my socks.

"I feel like I can't go to the playground anymore!" I complained to Tati one Shabbos afternoon soon after my Bar Mitzvah. "I look different from everyone else, and I'll get my white socks dirty."

"Well, that is the point!" he said. "We have to be role models, we have to be extra careful with everything we do."

So the dress code identified us as VIPs, but it was also meant to keep us in line. We had to behave perfectly because we were boys of stature and men of holy importance. Just look at our socks and you can see!

I BEGAN TO have nightmares.

In one, I chased my little sister Miriam but could not catch her.

"Miriam, why are you running away from me?" I cried.

"You are a boy, but you are a strange boy," she replied. "You are a girl that is living like a boy, dressing like a boy, and that is scary. I am afraid I will end up like you!"

"But I don't have a choice!" I argued. "I want to live like a girl, but everyone says that I am a boy, and I have to follow along!"

"*Shtisim*," Miriam replied, using the Yiddish word for BS. "You have a choice, you are just not trying hard enough!"

"Please come back, Miriam. Tell me what to do, and I will do it, just come back!"

"You have to die, and only then you will be reborn as a real girl," she said. "It is easy, you can do it! Just jump off the balcony."

I walked to the balcony and considered her advice.

"You are right, Miriam. That is the only choice I have, to die and be reborn," I said.

I leaned toward the edge of the balcony, ready to leap.

Then I woke up in my bed, sweating and weeping.

I'd had nightmares before, but this was the worst. Hearing Miriam's voice telling me I scared her, and that I had to die, undid me.

Miriam loved me. We all loved each other. But Miriam and I were special to each other. In a family of thirteen, we naturally created closer ties with a chosen sibling, someone to watch over and attend to us when a parent couldn't. I was the only one other than Mommy who could get Miriam to fall asleep at night, and when she was fighting with one of our siblings, she would run to me to protect her.

So to dream she rejected me because I was not living like the girl I was—clearly a reflection of my own fears displaced on her—was painful.

Facing death because she encouraged me to do so was horrifying.

I had that dream the night I turned thirteen, the night of my Bar Mitzvah, when I was supposed to become "a man."

AT THREE, MY hair was cut and I was dressed in princely robes.

At thirteen, I became a *bar mitzvah*, and began wearing a man's long white knee socks and a fur hat.

And with my thirteenth birthday also came puberty. I had noticed my first facial hairs, a feathering of soft, fine hair on my neck, in the weeks leading up to my birthday. I had also begun to have my first sexual feelings. I had not been taught about sex, either at school or at home; there wasn't even a need to preach abstinence because it was assumed boys and girls would not touch—let alone kiss or have intercourse—until they were married. But the feelings were there, regardless, and I was confused.

I started looking at boys differently, noticing which ones were cute. Confusing the matter, I noticed girls, too, though less so—most of my fantasies were about marrying a boy. All of this, combined with the preparations for my Bar Mitzvah, had amped up my gender discomfort to a whole new level.

"The Tefillin are holy," Tati said. "So holy that only men, who have purer bodies, can wear them." He was explaining to me why women never wore them. Tefillin is a biblical ritual object: the leather boxes have handwritten Bible texts in them, and leather straps are used to wrap them around the arm and the forehead. In the Orthodox world, men wear them every weekday morning. Soon, I would wear them, too.

That obviously did not make me feel better.

Everywhere I turned, I bumped into signs and signals that I was becoming a man.

One Friday night, a week before my Bar Mitzvah, Tati sent me to bed early.

"You have to wake up early," Tati told me. "You should go to the *mikvah* before morning prayers. You are becoming an adult, so you should do what all adult men do!"

The mikvah is a ritual bath that Jews have used for purification since the time of the Temple in Jerusalem. While in most religious Jewish communities the mikvah is used mostly by women to "purify" themselves every month after their periods, and after giving birth, in the Hasidic community men use it more often. Every big Hasidic synagogue has its own mikvah, and the custom is for men to immerse themselves in the water every day.

I actually loved the mikvah. It was like taking a warm bath every morning, which is a great way to wake up. Boys are permitted to go before they turn thirteen, but they usually go before Shabbos on Friday afternoon, not on Saturday morning. But that morning, for the first time, I went with Tati to the mikvah on Shabbos. As I walked into synagogue afterward, with my payos still wet, I bumped into a family friend. "A *child* going to the mikvah on Shabbos?! How is that okay?" he joked.

He intended to tease me because I was not yet thirteen. But to me, he was right, I should not have been using the mikvah— but not because I was too young. I should not have gone because I was a girl, and girls do not use the mikvah until they get married.

I shrugged off his remark, pretending it did not affect me, but I could not escape the sound of his voice, the truth he'd unwittingly stumbled upon. It echoed in my ears for the rest of the day.

I had gone to the mikvah, pretending I was a boy. I sat with the men in synagogue, close to the Torah, instead of with the women behind the curtain in the back, pretending I would soon be a man.

I noticed these disconnects everywhere. I found them in every step.

I tried to make sense of it all, to translate for myself the *boy* into *girl*. I sat in synagogue and looked at my *veise zoken*, imagining they were not white socks but long tights, just like the ones my sisters wore.

Yes, Mommy, it's a girlish thing.

8

HOLY OBLIGATIONS

"**D**ID YOU LOSE your mind altogether?" Tati screamed. "How could you be so disrespectful to Reb Shimon?"

"He made me angry, and he hates me for no good reason!" I screamed back. "And anyway, you know I never wanted to stay in yeshiva!"

"So that is your excuse for your rudeness?" Tati screamed back. His eyes were wild. I had never seen him so angry.

"I don't belong there!" I cried. "Or in any yeshiva! I don't care about any of it!"

"What did you just say?!" Now Tati wasn't just angry, he was shocked.

"You heard me! I *do not care!*"

For a half a minute neither of us said anything. We stood and glared at each other in the pounding silence.

Then Tati picked up his hand and hit me on my face. Hard. Another smack. And another.

I ran out of the house.

As I left, I passed Mommy. "I am never coming back!" I seethed to her.

It was the end of the winter semester. By that time, instead of high school, Hasidic boys attended yeshiva, a seminary with an intense religious curriculum.

The yeshiva weekday for teenagers, in most Hasidic schools, is filled with studies from morning until night, without much downtime or rest. Based on biblical verses and rabbinic teachings, a Hasidic Jew has an inherent obligation not to waste a single minute of the day. "*Bittul Torah*," a phrase used to describe anything that gets in the way of studying, is a concept Hasidic boys are lectured about from a young age. Yes, yeshivas allow students to take breaks for food, sleep, and an opportunity to unwind, but it is all just for one goal—so that the student can return to his studies refreshed.

The school day started at around 6:00 in the morning, when we were supposed to be in the study hall with our textbooks, ready to study.

At 8:00 a.m. we took a short break to prepare for morning prayers. We could grab a second (or often, a third) cup of coffee—most yeshivas provide free coffee all day long—and then use the bathrooms to make sure our bodies were "clean," a requirement before putting on Tefillin.

At 8:15 we prayed. The morning prayer liturgy is the longest and most important set of daily prayers. While in most synagogues the average length for weekday morning prayers is about forty minutes, in my yeshiva it lasted more than an hour.

"If, as a teenager, your morning praying takes you an hour," I remember Reb Klar, my ninth-grade teacher telling us, "then we can expect that once you are married, and you have a busy life outside of studying, it will take you forty-five minutes. But if in yeshiva it takes you forty-five minutes, then God forbid, when you are older, it will take just a few minutes!"

As teenagers, we were expected to take the prayers more seriously than ever before, and to pray with intensity, focusing on connecting to the Divine. "Anyone who does not pray with full dedication to the prayers will feel that whole day that it affects his ability to study Torah as he is supposed to!" we were told.

I was now questioning everything I was supposed to believe, and forging a connection to a divine presence I didn't believe in wasn't going to happen. Instead, community prayer time gave me an opportunity to act out, to irritate the rabbis. You see, the members of every Hasidic sect have their own unique way of chanting prayers that differentiate them from all the others. Viznitz stands out from the rest, with special tunes for the chanted prayers that are believed to date back to the Baal Shem Tov. While this might sound like minutiae to outsiders, in the Hasidic world, where everything is so unified, a Viznitz tune is always noticeable. So although I could not enjoy praying to get closer to the Divine, I could enjoy it in other ways. While the rabbis and other students crooned the blessings to one tune, I warbled loudly with another, defying anyone who tried to stop my fervent supplications and get with the program.

What can I say? I was a teenager. I reveled in being annoying.

After morning prayers, we had forty-five minutes or so to eat breakfast. Most days we were served a continental-style breakfast, with eggs, tuna, bread and toast, and vegetables. It was tasty, and it was my favorite meal of the day at school.

After breakfast came the morning study session, which lasted until 2:00 p.m. The session was dedicated to studying Talmud using a form of learning called *Sheir Eyin*, which literally means "deep study session." Our cohort of students and rabbis would read the Talmud, line by line, word by word, and dissect every possible meaning, every implication, every possible interpretation. It could take us a week to cover half a page.

The rabbis told us to treat it as though we were treading water, staying in one place and engaging in one action.

I found it maddening. In order to stay in one place and not ask the same questions over and over, we created unnecessary questions just so we could answer them. In other words, we were finding ways *not* to understand the Talmud, just so we could then try to understand it. It wasn't enough just to read it, take in its meaning, and move on, questioning only what arose as complicated or essential.

One day during the first week of classes, we were—once again—studying the laws of divorce, as outlined in the tractate of Gittin. The Mishna explores the legal quirks of a bill of divorce issued by a court outside of Israel. At the time, the courts from outside the land of Israel were considered slightly less trustworthy, and therefore in need of extra scrutiny. If the bill of divorce was issued from one of these outside courts, but still needed to be enforced in Israel, the messenger was instructed to bear witness, and to recite a legal term that assured the court in Israel that it had been written and signed in accordance with Jewish law. As part of this exploration, it must be clear which cities were considered to be within the realm of Israel and which were not.

The Mishna gives a few examples of cities on the border of Israel and states whether they were considered to be part of Israel or not. Through these examples, we could draw lines on a map and find the exact borders of Israel, at least insofar as what was considered Israel for matters of divorce.

"So, let us consider," Reb Shimon said, "what could be the reason why the Mishna specifically mentions these particular places?"

I raised my hand. "They are examples of cities that lie near the border." Easy.

"Well, yes," Reb Shimon responded. "But why does it mention *these* specific cities?"

"Well, as I have said, I think these are just examples," I said. Then, with a smirk on my face, I added, "If they had chosen other examples, you would ask why they used those!"

Instead of dignifying my quip with a response, Reb Shimon went on, asking us to decide why these cities in particular were so important.

How could they be important if their geographic value no longer existed? I wanted to roll my eyes.

"So, let me get this straight," I said instead, without raising my hand. "I think these are just examples, with no further meaning. But you are saying they were intentionally chosen. Maybe you are right, but maybe I am. What if they really are just examples? What if there is no meaning to them? Why are we asking ourselves these questions, over and over, when we will never know the original intention of our ancestors and the answer doesn't have any consequence?"

By now Reb Shimon's annoyance had peaked and was turning into anger. "This is what deep studying is all about!" he responded. "We learn by asking questions and seeking answers!"

"If you ask me, this isn't deep studying. Deep studying would be trying to understand what is important, what is meaningful.

Why do we need to create a problem, and a small one at that, just so we can spend a few hours trying to solve it?"

"Are you saying that our entire form of studying is stupid?" Reb Shimon said. He was furious now, his face red.

"Exactly!" I exclaimed.

"How dare you!" he shouted back. "You are questioning the holy teachings of our rabbis!"

His voice was loud, the classroom was quiet, and everyone's eyes were on me.

The truth was that, yes, I was questioning our rabbis. I questioned everything. I knew that questioning the authority of the rabbis was heresy, and that this would not end well for me, but at the same time I couldn't pretend I believed that a world that called me a boy, when I was so thoroughly a girl, had a monopoly on truth. I was silent for a minute.

"Of course not," I said, finally. "I am simply asking why we are asking the same questions over and over, for hours at a time and year after year, about something insignificant that was written eighteen hundred years ago." There, that was better.

Or maybe it wasn't.

"That is heresy!" Reb Shimon exclaimed, and then added, "Where do you get such smartass opinions?"

AT 2:00 WE had an hour for lunch, and the afternoon study period started at 3:00. In that session, we studied *Shulchan Aruch*, the sixteenth-century Jewish law code. To this day it is the go-to source for Jewish law in all Orthodox, Conservative, Sephardic, and many other religious communities. In yeshiva we started to study the laws of Shabbos, the single biggest and most complex part of commonly studied Jewish law. For me, that was the beginning of my study for rabbinical ordination.

At some point in the middle of afternoon studies we would break for *Mincha*, afternoon prayers, and then we continued studying until 6:15.

At 6:15 there was a short fifteen-minute break, when we had a chance to go to the dining hall, eat some cookies, and drink more coffee. Coffee was always popular at night. It gave us the energy we needed to get through our next stretch of studying.

Then came the evening study session, from 6:30 until 7:45. The evening study time was quite relaxed. Instead of the teacher giving a class in the classroom, we would sit and study in the study hall, on our own or with a partner.

Then we went home, ate dinner, and went to bed.

The cycle repeated, Monday through Thursday. On Sundays, there was no early-morning study session; instead we began our day with morning prayers at the decadently late hour of 9:15. A few students would arrive as late as 10:30, having skipped our communal recitation of the morning prayers in favor of sleeping later and praying on their own.

I almost never skipped the morning prayers, and I would guess that about 90 percent of Hasidic boys do not miss a single day once they turn thirteen.

The second Sunday in the school year was the first time I ever skipped morning prayers.

I had woken up just a bit late. Usually I'd get up at 8:30, take five minutes to dress, and then walk to the ritual bath. After the mikvah, I'd go to yeshiva to get there in time for the start of morning prayers. But that Sunday, I woke up at 9:00. Many boys would not think twice before skipping the ritual bath for just one day, but I loved it, so instead of going straight to yeshiva, I went instead to the bath, knowing that I would miss prayer time.

It's no big deal, I thought. *I will just immerse in the bath, and then I will pray at the local synagogue.*

The bath was small and beautifully designed, with blue tiles that made the water look like the ocean. The water was as warm as a heated swimming pool, and I submerged myself into it, enjoying the sensation. Being there alone, I realized I had a few extra minutes to think—a rare, quiet moment of solitude. I should have hurried—I was already late—but instead I lingered with my thoughts.

Time passed. I was missing morning prayers.

What am I doing? I asked myself. *Do I really believe there is a God who cares if I immerse myself in the bath before prayers, or will care if I pray at all?* My thoughts went further. *Is there really a God who hears those prayers? Or am I just saying words but no one is listening?*

These questions were considered *machshovos zoros*—foreign thoughts, evil thoughts.

That morning I took my time. After half an hour in the mikvah, I slowly dressed and left for the yeshiva. Instead of taking the fastest route, I chose another path, one that took me close to the edge of our neighborhood, where secular New Yorkers passed. We had been warned many times not to go there, that it was a road to be avoided. But it gave me twenty minutes to walk and think as I made my way along Kent Avenue, adjacent to the Brooklyn Navy Yard.

My mind was arguing with itself over missing my prayers, full of conflict and dissonance. As I strode under the BQE and passed a non-Jewish couple walking with their children, regret and shame arose inside of me: *We are the chosen people. I am obligated to honor our holy existence. I should have prayed.* Then another voice, one that had been in my consciousness since I was a child, argued back: *If I don't pray, then maybe I am not so special after all—I am just as unimportant as a non-Jew.*

I finally calmed my inner voices with a new thought. *I am a girl*, I reminded myself, *and girls are not obligated to pray three times a day.*

My heart stopped pounding, and I breathed easier. My guilt was assuaged with what I knew to be true. No matter what those inner voices argued, there was one thing we could all agree on: I was a girl.

After that, I missed prayers many times. It was an infraction of our tradition, but it was not a sin.

I did not break the Shabbos or eat non-kosher food—those were laws that girls are obligated to follow, and so I did. And if an inner voice came nagging, I reminded it that I was a girl and living a holy life.

It was all good.

9

TEACHINGS OF OUR FATHERS

"**AM I GOING** to go to Shopron again next year?" I asked Tati one summer afternoon in ninth grade.

Tati, Mommy, Hershy, and I were walking down the big mountain from our bungalow to the kosher grocery. Every summer since Tati had started teaching in Shopron Yeshiva in 1990, my family had spent the summer months at the school's campground in the Catskills.

Shopron was a beautiful camp, situated in the heart of what used to be called the Borscht Belt, the summer colonies where New York's Jews, secular and religious, spent their summers. During the 1970s and 1980s, non-Orthodox Jews deserted the Borscht Belt in the thousands, which left the place open for the Hasidic community to come in and buy out all the hotels and colonies. Today, more than half of the New York City Hasidic community spends their summers in the Catskills.

For my brothers and me, camp meant enjoying being kids. The rest of our classmates slept in bunks away from their families, but we stayed with our parents, ate in our bungalow, and spent leisurely afternoons together in a beautiful mountainous setting.

"Why would you not stay at the school?" Mommy asked.

I gave her a look that said, *You know why.*

Then I turned to Tati, my eyes now saying, *Help me out here.* Tati didn't.

"You are a good student, right?" Tati said. "I don't see why my being your teacher should be a problem."

Yes, Tati was the afternoon tenth-grade teacher. That meant I'd have my father as my teacher from 3:00 to 8:00 p.m. every day. I doubt any teenager would be happy about that, but I was especially uncomfortable with it. I might have been a good student, but I loved causing trouble. It was my outlet. I was always subtle with my hijinks, and I could usually get away with it in front of most teachers. But it would be a lot harder, and far more awkward, when that teacher was Tati. *Oh well*, I thought. *How bad can it be?*

It didn't take long to find out.

School started the week after Sukkos 5766 (fall 2005), and right away we delved into deep study, the kind I hated. It made me impatient, and I'd get distracted. I was eager to find a way to show that just because my father was the afternoon teacher, that didn't mean I would be the teacher's pet. By the second week, my urge to rebel was just under the surface. The semester dragged and eventually headed straight into a depressing winter.

Every day was a struggle. My inner self was growing more and more at odds with my outside existence as the onslaught of male puberty messed with my body and my mind. I desperately needed an outlet, and the only outlet I had was to disrupt those around me.

All the while, I had one constant enemy: my morning teacher, Reb Shimon. I had no respect for him or for what he was teaching, and I looked for ways to irritate him. There was always kind of a friendly rivalry between the students who preferred the morning teacher and the students who preferred the afternoon one, and I had a perfect excuse to take my father's side. No matter what I did during the morning sessions, I behaved perfectly whenever Tati was around. Meanwhile, Reb Shimon never wanted Tati to think of him as so weak that he couldn't control his students, so he rarely told him about the trouble I caused.

And I did cause trouble.

Reb Shimon had a microphone in class and he didn't want us using it. Our classroom was large, with six tables placed in a wide U shape. Four students sat at each table, and at the open end of the U, in the front of the room, was a podium where Reb Shimon stood while teaching. He used the microphone to project his lessons around the room. We could hear him just fine without it, but he always used it, as if we were an audience of three hundred instead of a class of twenty-four.

I could only guess that Reb Shimon thought the microphone projected authority: it was a common practice among Hasidic schoolteachers. Since second grade, all of our teachers had sat on stages, reinforcing the power structure of the classroom—the teacher is up high, and the students are down low. It annoyed me. And one day, I came up with a plan that seemed like the perfect way to stir up trouble and subvert the power structure. It would demean Reb Shimon, and at the same time, in my fourteen-year-old mind, it would uplift Tati.

The best part of it all: I could do it without anyone knowing. Which made it the perfect crime.

One afternoon, while everyone was in the study hall, I went to the empty classroom. Right next to the door, on a shelf welded to the wall, were the controls for Reb Shimon's microphone. Every morning, he would walk into the classroom, flip a switch to turn on the microphone's speaker, and make his way to the front of the room. The volume knob was preset; he never touched it.

That afternoon, after making sure no one in the hall could see me, I snuck into the classroom and turned all the knobs to their highest settings and left.

The next morning, just before Reb Shimon entered the class-room, I went to the bathroom. I knew what was going to happen and wasn't sure I'd be able to act surprised. The bathroom was about 150 feet away from the classrooms, and I lingered there, waiting for the burst of loud noise.

And loud it was! It was one of the loudest sounds I have ever heard. It screeched through the halls and in the stairwells. I imagine the entire building could hear it.

I headed back into the classroom, prepared to act astonished. I adjusted my face into a "What happened?" expression and en-tered the room. Reb Shimon's face was bright red, and he was fuming. It wasn't just the class disruption that upset him—it was the fact that he'd been publicly embarrassed.

The class was chuckling and smirking; even the best-behaved students were enjoying the uproar. I almost felt bad for him.

Reb Shimon ordered us to be silent.

"I assume whoever did this did it by mistake," he said. "Who-ever did it, come talk to me after class, and I will forgive you." He set the volume back to its original setting and began teaching.

I knew he meant it, that he would forgive whoever did it, and that his primary concern was finding out who it was. He needed to know so he could regain control, even if it meant overlooking an opportunity for punishment.

Of course, no one took responsibility. I felt a satisfying rise; yes, I pitied him, but it made me feel accomplished to have some control, just for a moment, over my life. And the heresy that was brewing in my mind was sustained, too. *Studying Torah the whole day is a waste of time anyway*, I thought.

That next day, I did the same thing again. This time, I was sitting at my place in the classroom when Reb Shimon walked in. My designated spot was in one of the seats closest to the door, a spot I had chosen at the beginning of the term so I wouldn't have to be in front of Tati's gaze when he was teaching in the afternoons. Now, however, it meant sitting right next to the speaker.

Again, Reb Shimon flipped the on switch, made his way to the front of the room, and spoke into the microphone. Again, the speakers emitted a loud, screeching scream. Many of my classmates, myself included, screamed, startled by the sudden piercing in our ears. In all honesty, I was surprised myself by how loud it was, and my reaction was entirely authentic.

This time, Reb Shimon lost it, big-time.

"Whoever is doing this is not just showing immense disrespect to me as a teacher, but also to the whole Torah and to this whole class and school!" he fumed. "And to God!" he went on. "This person has no *yiras shamayim*, no respect for the Divine, and no respect for Judaism! The punishment for that, in this world and in the world to come, is beyond comprehension. His sin is bigger than anyone could carry!"

I had to agree with him. He was right: I had no respect for the school, or for the Divine. I wasn't proud of it, but it was the truth. We all sat, hushed and exchanging an occasional glance, as Reb Shimon stormed out of the room.

A few minutes later, he returned with a cup of coffee. He reset the volume knob to the proper level and began the lesson.

The next morning, I did it again. The scream of the speakers filled the room and carried down the hall. After our initial reaction, the classroom went quiet, and we all froze. Reb Shimon sat down at the desk at the front of the room and spoke.

"I imagine that whoever is doing this heinous act is broken. Only a student who feels broken and lost would do something like this, and I pity that student," he said. He went on like this for about half an hour, lecturing us about anger and broken souls and their influence on our spiritual and physical lives.

He finally finished with the ultimate threat.

"If the student who did this will not come talk to me and admit his sins, I will never forgive him. I will not forgive him in this life, in any other life, or in the world to come. And it is not just him I will not forgive but everyone who knows who the student is who has committed this act. God will punish you all, and I will never forgive any of you!"

If only the person he was speaking about believed in the Divine, his threat would have worked. Unfortunately for him, he was speaking about me.

I did it again the next day.

This time, though, he checked the settings before he began to teach. The game was over.

I was kind of relieved.

But that didn't mean I was ready to change my ways.

In our school, there was a natural rivalry between the ninth and tenth grades. We were only a year apart, but ninth grade was still considered grade school while we were in yeshiva. In the Hasidic educational hierarchy, we were a world apart. Ninth-grade students are still kids; yeshiva students are adults. Teenagers, yes, but adults.

Most of the time, the rivalry played out with run-of-the-mill teasing, the tenth graders picking on the ninth graders. When they were in their classroom without a teacher, for instance, we would throw things at the ninth graders through their window. It started out with water, then toilet paper rolls, then leftover food from the dining hall—or anything else that wouldn't physically harm anyone. We were jokesters, not barbarians! Still, the school's administration constantly got complaints, and from time to time we'd get yelled at by the teachers and principal. No one was really punished. After all, in a community where there are no sports, a bit of (not so) friendly rivalry was not such a terrible thing.

Then, one afternoon, all of the yeshiva students went on a class trip to visit a rabbi in upstate New York. With the tenth graders away, the ninth graders saw an opportunity. When we got back to the yeshiva building, behold, we found the entire classroom vandalized. The usually clean yellow tables were covered in leftover greasy food. All six windows were draped in toilet paper, and on the floor, there was a mix of water and cocoa. It was a disaster zone.

The next day, the window fights became harsher than ever.

This time, armed with tissues soaked in sticky sugar water, our class bombarded their windows with renewed force. Leading the pack was Moishy, a sweaty six-foot-tall boy and the uncrowned general of our inter-grade wars. As he hurled globs of wet tissue, I came up with an idea.

Now, to be clear, I wasn't among the students who were engaged in the armed warfare. Given my status as a good student and my father's child, I couldn't take part in the fighting. But I was itching to be seen and itching to rebel.

"Hey, Moishy!" I called out to him as he walked by the library where I was standing while watching the battlefield.

"Yeah?"

"You know the coffee we have in our coffee room?" I said. We always had two kinds, Nescafé and Taster's Choice. "When you mix coffee, sugar, and hot water, it becomes a sticky mush that looks and kind of smells like poop! And it sticks really well to skin and clothes," I informed him.

So Moishy, together with a few other students, went to the coffee room and made a few cups of the nasty mix. Then they went back to the classroom window, and after a minute, I could hear the screams of the ninth graders in the study hall.

"Poop! It's poop!" they screamed.

Chaos erupted. "Poop" was everywhere—it seemed like the more the ninth graders tried to clean it up, the more it spread. At one point a boy got it in his eye and shrieked in pain; apparently coffee grounds mixed with water and sugar do not make for a concoction that is easy on the eyes. He was fine, but his parents had to take him to the doctor.

This was too much for the administration to ignore.

That afternoon, the principal came into our classroom shouting. "That's it! You all went too far this time! If this ever happens again, I will find the student who made this mix and I will expel him!"

I was invigorated.

The next day, at lunch, I again called to Moishy and a few of his soldiers. "Are you really going to let ninth grade get away with this? They still have not paid enough for what they did," I pointed out. "Besides, the Talmud says that you have to respect your elders, and it is our obligation to teach them respect. It is our mitzvah!" Then, just for a final touch, I quoted the Talmud with a line that roughly means: "I am just doing this out of religious obligation."

But before we could plot a second insurgence, a guest showed up in our school: Miriam Meisels, the rabbi's wife, and, by extension, Zeide Meisels' first cousin by marriage and Tati's sister's mother-in-law. She'd been brought to school as the big gun, so to speak. She was a master detective, and was called in whenever the administration needed to get something out of the students that they refused to tell. Every student at Shopron was terrified of her. She had full authority to expel students at a whim, and it was clear that she was going to figure out who was behind this. In all likelihood, that student would be expelled.

An hour or so after the investigation started, it became clear that she was not concerned with the students who had thrown the coffee mix, but with the mastermind who had plotted it. She was after the head of the snake. She was after me.

I was sure that my hours at the school were limited.

As Miriam Meisels questioned all the students, I took stock of my situation. I had no real friends, and if there is one kind of boy that teenagers love to mess with, it's the freak, the weakling, the boy that is too girlish. I couldn't expect Moishy and the others to protect me; in fact, I'd be the perfect excuse for them to get out of trouble themselves.

After some time, I saw the principal enter the study hall and call Tati into his office.

A few minutes later, I was called in, too.

The principal's office, intentionally or unintentionally, was a menacing room. Large and ominous, it had exposed brick and metal pipes and was dimly lit. There was a large, half-broken mahogany table at one end, a metal bookcase and two metal chairs at the other end, and that's it.

In the room was Tati, angry, talking with Miriam Meisels. They both turned to look at me.

"When I came here today, I was sure that when I found the student responsible for that dangerous mix, I would kick him out of school," Miriam Meisels said in a quiet scream. "I was expecting it to be a troublemaker, not you! A child of a rabbinic family, one of our best students, and my relative on top of that!"

I probably should have hung my head. Instead, I just stood there, waiting for the ax to fall.

But then she said, "I'm not going to expel you. Instead I have worked out a punishment with your father. You have to commit to taking on an additional subject of study, something not studied by other students, and you have to study it at lunch every day. Every week, in addition to the standard exams on all the schoolwork, you will be examined on that topic as well."

I wanted to burst out laughing. That was my punishment? An excuse to read during lunchtime? Sure, I'd do it. I tried to look repentant, but inside I was chuckling.

Throughout my childhood, showing off and being unique were not just a way to stand out, but also a way to express on the outside the discomfort I felt internally.

"I love you, you know that, right?" Zeide Stein said one day, after I'd caused another uproar in school. This time I had decided to go "all Viznitz," to fully embrace the Viznitz Hasidic sect, customs, and beliefs, a rebellious stance in a Satmar school. And I had made two bold changes that publicly emphasized my Viznitz stance.

The first change, and the easier one for Tati to deal with, was the way I wore my hat. All Hasidic communities other than Viznitz wear their hats with the bow on the left side. Viznitz Hasidim, however, in a custom dating back before the war, wear their hats with the bow on the right side. This may sound like an insignificant detail, but in yeshiva, it is a striking way of announcing to everyone, "I am Viznitz, and I am different from all of you."

Tati did his best to sway me back to the left side, and he even tried forcing me, but after a while he gave up. He had to choose his battles.

Then there was the approach to Israel, however.

Satmar Hasidim are staunchly anti-Zionist. Not just anti-Israel as it stands today, but opposed to the idea of Jews having a state in the land of Israel before the Messiah comes, riding on a white donkey from heaven. They agree that Israel is the holy land, and the homeland of the Jewish people, and even in Satmar it is common to refer to Israel as "Our Holy Land." But they believe that Jews should not have a state until it is given to us from heaven, a principle of faith. Satmar Hasidim consider people who support Israel to be heretics, akin to people who deny the world to come. Supporting Israel in any way is considered a kind of heresy that excludes you from being counted as a faithful Jew.

Viznitz Hasidim have a laxer opinion about Israel. They take issue with the fact that the current Israeli government is

not religious enough, and that it doesn't respect all the Orthodox laws, and instead allows other religions, such as Islam and
Christianity, to exist in Israel. But the basic idea of a Jewish state
they (kind of) don't mind.

The Satmar Rebbe wrote a book called *V'yoel Moshe* in which
he laid out his religious and theological opposition to Israel.
Among Satmar Hasidism, that book is like a Bible. They study
it, sanctify it, and teach from it as if it were the Torah or the
Talmud. There was a weekly class on it in the yeshiva, but we
were not required to attend. I opted out.

One day, my cousin Shimon Yisroel Meisels passed me on
the way to class. "Why aren't you going to the class?" he asked.

"*V'yoel Moshe* is a coloring book," I responded, as if to say it
was silly and not worth my time.

Shimon Yisroel went off to class and repeated it to a few other
students, and all hell broke loose. For the next few days, no one
spoke to me. Then the principal tried talking to me, to explain to
me how disrespectful my words were.

"But I am a Viznitz Hasid, so I don't care what Satmar people
think about it!" I responded.

When it became clear that I was not going to recant, and that
I was willing to be treated like a pariah in school, Tati decided
to bring in Zeide Stein.

"Tell me, please, why do you insist on being so different?"
he asked. "You know that I love that you are so dedicated to
Viznitz. You remind me of me as a teenager. But I am deeply
worried. It's not healthy for you to be so on your own, and to
fight back so strongly against your classmates."

I knew he meant what he said, that he loved me, and that he
was legitimately worried, as Tati and Mommy were, that I was

hiding something existential, something that was causing me to act out.

"I don't know why," I said. "It just feels good to stand out."

I was lying, of course. I knew why. I was a girl, and it felt good to show everyone that I did not belong with the boys.

I couldn't tell Zeide that, though.

FOR THE REST of the semester, my behavior wavered. Some days I was the perfect student, studying and praying as I was expected to. Other days I claimed I was sick so I could avoid going to that dreaded school at all. And then there were the days when I acted out, either with low-key bad behavior or high-key religious disagreements with my teachers.

Then it reached a boiling point.

We were in the last two weeks of the winter semester, a time when the yeshiva is the most relaxed. One morning, a mystery student mixed that coffee-sugary poop recipe I invented and somehow got it onto Reb Shimon. I don't know who did it or how, but Reb Shimon was convinced I was to blame.

He walked into the study hall, right over to where I was sitting, and screamed, "Get out of here and meet me in the classroom! You are not getting away with it this time!"

Taken aback, I protested. "But I didn't do anything!"

"We both know you did!" Reb Shimon retorted. His face was reddening, he was sweating, and it looked as though he were about to hit me. I stood up and followed him to the door, my own anger rising.

I shouted back at him, "You are just picking on me because of my father! Everyone knows that he is a better teacher and you are just jealous!"

Everyone in the study hall heard me, and it got very quiet.

Reb Shimon froze, seething. I have never seen an adult so angry; he looked like a child throwing a temper tantrum. I strode away from him toward the classroom.

Reb Shimon caught up to me in the hallway.

Then he slapped me in the face.

Then he slapped me again. This time it was so loud that my classmates could hear it in the study hall.

"You are a misfit!" Reb Shimon yelled. "A misfit with the biggest amount of misplaced chutzpah!" he screamed. "Nothing good will ever come of you if you cannot take responsibility for your actions!"

He slapped me again, and again.

"I have put up with your shenanigans out of respect for your father, but no more. I am not doing you or your family any favors by letting you get away with it. Admit what you did!"

"No, no, no, and no!" I screamed back. "I have nothing to admit to because I didn't do anything!"

He slapped me again. And again.

I realized that he was not going to stop until I said I did it. Which I wouldn't do.

I tried to turn around and run away, but he caught my feet, knocked me over, and jabbed me in the stomach with his feet as I lay on the floor. I started to cry.

"Are you crying, baby?" he mocked me. "Well, I am not going to stop until you admit to what you did!"

I crawled into a corner and cried louder.

Everyone could hear me, and we both knew it. Taken aback by my sobs, he took a few steps backward, and I took advantage of the opportunity. I stood up, ran down the hallway, and stopped before I reached the door. I turned around, faced him, and looked him straight in the eye.

"You are crazy—crazy and twisted!" I shouted with my last breath. *"And everyone knows it!"*

I ran to the door, out the building, and down the street, running for blocks, terrified that he would follow and hit me again.

I got home, and Mommy already knew what had happened.

A little after that, Tati came home, full of anger.

Then Tati hit me.

AFTER A FEW hours, we all calmed down.

I apologized to Tati and convinced him that I really had not done it, and I told him that Reb Shimon had physically harmed me, showing him the bruises on my stomach.

I started crying again.

"Okay, stop it, you are crying like a girl," Tati said. "I believe you. We will figure something out," he said lovingly. Then he hugged me, something he rarely did.

It soon became clear that I would have to change schools. But where would we find a school in the middle of the year?

10

A NEW SCHOOL

"THERE IS NOTHING I can do to influence his mind," Reb Mendel Meir Yakovovitz said with a sigh. "He thinks he is smarter than everyone."

It was the winter semester of 2008—or 5768, as I knew it—and I was in my third year of yeshiva when my teacher, Reb Yakovovitz, called Tati and me to the school to discuss my future.

"Well, Reb Mendel Meir," Tati responded, "two years ago, when Rabbi Chaim Shia Rubin was still his principal, he called me once after talking with my son and said, 'He is like a living orphan. His parents might still be alive, but his opinions are all his own!' I guess he was right," Tati joked with a funny smirk on his face.

I think there was a part of him that was proud of me and my questioning mind.

All three of us were quiet for a minute. Finally, Reb Yakovovitz turned to me.

"And what do you have to say to all of this?" he asked.

I had been sitting up straight at the small table, my hands on my crossed legs, with a reactionless face. Now I changed my posture, leaning my head on my hand as if I were half awake, to make it clear that I could not care less. Then I murmured, "Well, in all honesty, I am proud of myself. Being an independent thinker is a good thing, even when you make it sound like it isn't."

"Okay, okay, we are getting carried away here," Tati jumped in. "Let's get back to logistics. How can we make sure that everyone is satisfied—you as the teacher, and my child as a *mevakesh*?"

Tati took my side here, kind of. *Mevakesh* is a Hebrew term for a seeker, usually referring to young people who go out of their way to find the right spiritual and religious path for themselves. It does come with a slightly negative connotation, a hint that the young person can't just follow the traditional path the way he should. For a community that values obedience, this didn't reflect well on me. Still, some amount of respect was reserved for the seeker who was devoted to asking questions and seeking higher wisdom.

I was grateful to Tati for trying to put me in a good light, and it seemed to make an impression on Reb Yakovovitz, too.

"We will try again," he said, giving me a wary look from under his eyebrows. "We will all try."

AFTER THE INCIDENT with Reb Shimon at Shopron, Tati began his hunt for a new yeshiva for me.

Tati had been swayed by my crying, my promises that I would behave better, and my convincing case that Reb Shimon had been wrong to hit me—with an added coda that "the whole semester he wanted me to fail because I am your son"—and we were all in agreement. My parents, along with Zeide Stein, with whom Tati constantly consulted, all believed I was a strong student and generally well behaved, and that the problem at Shopron was that it was difficult to excel when your father was one of your teachers.

It also helped my case that Tati and Reb Shimon were not fond of each other. They had a good working relationship, but Tati had little respect for Reb Shimon. Tati felt Reb Shimon's clothes were too modern—he wore a hat with a fold on the top and a bluish, short-jacketed suit—and that his teaching style was unproductive. As for Reb Shimon, he saw Tati as a privileged royal rabbinic child who only had his job because of his family status.

Still, although Reb Shimon had been wrong to hit me, he was far from wrong about his general assessment. I was in fact an unruly student. At one point, he put it this way: "His place is not in yeshiva." For once, I agreed with him.

But what else could I do?

"Would you want to switch to Tzhelim Yeshiva for next semester?" Tati asked one evening as we were on our way to synagogue for the Passover service. It was the start of the holiday, two weeks after the turbulent end to the winter semester in Shopron.

Tzhelim was one of the few pluralistic yeshivas in Williamsburg—not in the modern sense, but in the Hasidic context. It contained a mix of different Hasidic sects instead of being dominated by just one.

Tzhelim itself was not a sect, but it was one of the first major Hasidic communities to develop in Williamsburg in 1938. The rebbe of the Tzhelim community did not ascribe to a particular sect—an unusual status—and he established a yeshiva of all followers. There were a lot of Satmar families, of course, by virtue of the fact that it was in Williamsburg, but there were also members of sects that were too small to have their own yeshivas, including the Bobov, Viznitz, Boyan, and Stolin sects.

For me, that meant finally being in a school that was not dominated by Satmar, where I would not get into trouble just for being openly and proudly Viznitz. For the first time, I would be allowed to be different.

"I think I would love to go to Tzhelim!" I responded to Tati. "But are you sure you can get me in in the middle of the year?"

"Of course I can," Tati responded. "I already spoke to Mema Chaya, and she said it is all set."

Stupid me. Of course Tati could get me in. Or, rather, of course Mema Chaya could.

Mema Chaya, or, as she is known in the Hasidic world, Rebbetzin Chaya Greenwald, was a prolific and greatly admired speaker, but she was also one of Zeide Stein's three sisters. She was married to Rabbi Yosef Moshe Greenwald, the rebbe of the Tzhelim community, who was also quite well known, even to strangers and nonreligious Jews. This was because he gave the kosher certification for Kedem, Inc., the biggest kosher wine and grape juice producer and importer in the United States. His name is on every bottle of Kedem-branded wine and grape juice sold, and he is also responsible for the kosher certification for other wine manufacturers, such as Baron Herzog, Rashi, Geula, and every wine produced or imported under the Royal Wine Corporation name.

Mema Chaya was childless, despite decades of trying to conceive children of her own, and as a result many of her nieces and nephews became like sons and daughters to her. Tati, and in turn Mommy and the rest of us, were among those families. Mema Chaya and the Tzhelim'er Rebbe where like a third pair of grandparents to me and my siblings. We visited them on every holiday and family occasion, and we prayed at their synagogue a few times a year. Sometimes we would casually drop by their home for a visit, just like at Zeide and Bobbe's house.

I will never forget our visit to their house after my sister Miriam's birth. Miriam was born in the early morning hours of the final day of Passover in 2001, or 5761 by the Jewish calendar, and I was ten years old. Just a few weeks before that, Mommy had moved baby Suri's crib from her own room into one of the three bedrooms in our house to make room for a new infant who would soon be sleeping by her side. Our house was about to have more people living there than ever before—fourteen of us in all, two parents and twelve children. In fact, it was the most we would ever have: my parents actually had thirteen children, but by the time the youngest, Tzirel, was born, my oldest sister, Hannah Zissel, was married, and quite likely pregnant herself. It was not uncommon in our world for a mother and daughter to be pregnant at the same time.

In order to prevent overcrowding in the three children's bedrooms, my parents bought a new couch for our dining room, the largest room in the house. The couch had a full-size bed that could be pulled out at night and then folded up in the morning. I jumped at the opportunity to sleep there, and my parents agreed. In addition to the relative privacy it offered, it also meant I could leave the "boys' room" I'd been sharing with my brothers.

The final night of Passover, we ate our holiday meal at Zeide and Bobbe Meisels' house. The last day of Passover was always my favorite, as we got to eat the many delicious foods that were not permitted during the first seven days of the holiday. For instance, during those first seven days, we were not allowed to eat anything that was made outside of our own homes or one of our grandparents'. That meant no store-bought food, even foods that had been prepared as kosher for Passover, and no eating at other peoples' homes, including aunts and uncles. Hasidic people also do not eat "wet matzah" during the first seven days of Passover—that meant no matzah balls, no matzah meal pancakes or fried matzah, no matzah and cream cheese: indeed, almost all of the favorite matzah-based foods that so many Jews, religious and secular, enjoy on Passover are forbidden for Hasidic people.

There were some variations according to family and sect, of course: on Mommy's side of the family, for instance, women are exempted from the prohibition and are allowed to eat wet matzah. That custom had been established by the family patriarch, Rebbe Chaim Halberstam of Tzanz, one of the most popular Hasidic leaders of all time, who had lived in nineteenth-century Poland and was Mommy's direct ancestor. As part of the Jewish Enlightenment that was gaining traction in his time, there was a push for equality for women in the religious sphere. As a way of pushing back, Rebbe Chaim Halberstam enacted practices that had women even less involved. They were no longer obligated to eat in the sukkah or to fast on many of the traditional fast days, and they were permitted to eat wet matzah.

It was a kind of strange, reverse feminism. In the Hasidic world, the fewer rules women had to follow, the less holy and essential they were considered to be. These rules were so permissive on Mommy's side of the family that the women were jokingly called *tzanzer schmata*—a phrase that literally means "low-quality rags," but is colloquially used in Yiddish to describe items of low value.

Finally, though, on the last day of Passover, because it was only Passover according to rabbinic and not biblical law—in other words, the rabbis believed we should observe the holiday, but it was not written in the Torah—all of these restrictions were removed.

Every year we would go to Bobbe Meisels' house for the daytime meal, where the entire extended family would gather, bringing decadent foods like deep-fried matzah pancakes, fried and cooked matzah balls, cakes made out of layers of fried matzah, eggs covered with sugar, and other delicacies. After this sumptuous meal, we went home, had a lighter dinner, and went to sleep.

It must have been around three in the morning when I woke up to the sound of Mommy and Tati in the kitchen, right next to where I was sleeping in the dining room.

"Can we get a car to Wythe Avenue, please?" I heard Tati saying. "We are going to Beth Israel Hospital in Manhattan."

It took me a second to realize that—*gasp*—Tati was talking on the phone! On Shabbos and holidays, Orthodox Jews are not permitted to use anything with an electronic component—you can only use a telephone when someone is in danger. A woman in labor is considered to be in danger, but for a moment I forgot that Mommy was pregnant and I panicked. An emergency! Someone must be about to die, Tati was using the phone! Of course I knew that Mommy was pregnant, but it was rarely discussed, and in my half-awake state I had completely forgotten. Besides, the timelines of pregnancy were somewhat vague to us; I guess never being told how babies are born can do that to you.

I finally gathered my wits and realized that Mommy must be in labor. I heard Tati go into my sisters' room and wake up Hannah Zissel, who was sixteen at the time, to tell her what was happening. Then I heard Tati and Mommy leave, and Hannah Zissel come to the kitchen to recite psalms, the go-to prayers when something is wrong or when you are praying for someone's health.

At some point, I fell back asleep. I woke up again at around 8:00 a.m. to hear a knock on the door. I went to open it and it was Tati.

"Mazel tov!" he exclaimed with a smile. "Mommy had a girl baby!"

I shook Tati's hand in celebration, then kissed his hand, and he kissed my hand back, as was our family custom.

Mommy was known in the family for having very quick childbirths; her labors were always short and she had a knack for calculating the exact time she would need to arrive at the hospital. This time, however, the labor had been especially speedy, even for her. Mommy and Tati had left Williamsburg by car around 3:00 a.m., and by 8:00 a.m. Tati was already back home in Williamsburg after having walked home from the hospital. While some rabbis allow fathers to take a car back from the hospital after a birth on Shabbos and holidays, Tati followed the rule set by the Viznitz'er Rebbe: you can take a car going to the hospital, but not back, as your arrival is no longer considered a matter of danger. So he made his way home on foot, an hour-long trek through Manhattan and across the Williamsburg Bridge.

"Come with me, I want to go tell Mema Chaya the exciting news!" Tati said. He couldn't call his parents in Borough Park and tell them the good news until the end of the holiday that night, but he could at least tell his beloved aunt, who was almost like a second mother to him.

We left and walked to the Tzhelim synagogue where Mema Chaya and the Tzhelim'er Rebbe lived, just down the block from Zeide Meisels' synagogue on the corner of Bedford Avenue and Rodney Street. It was a nicely sized synagogue on the second floor of a prewar, castle-like red building. On the third floor was the women's section of the synagogue, and they lived on the fourth floor. We walked up to the fourth floor and knocked, but no one answered.

"Maybe she's still sleeping," I suggested.

"Nah, don't you know anything about Mema Chaya?" Tati said. "She prays three times a day, every day, in the synagogue, just like my Bobbe used to do." While most Hasidic men pray three times a day at synagogue, even once a day is rare for women. Only a handful of women go to synagogue three times a day. I knew that my great-grandmother, Tati's bobbe from Bensonhurst, did, and apparently Mema Chaya did the same.

So we went down a floor to the synagogue and peeked into the women's section. It was almost empty at such an early hour, but there were two or three older women there, including Mema Chaya.

"I can't go in. You go and ask her to come out," Tati said. It would be immodest for a man to enter the women's section, but since I was only ten, the offense would be small. I entered and went to Mema Chaya's side.

"My Tati wants to tell you something," I whispered. She grew pale and looked worried.

"Is he outside?" she asked, quickly standing up. She came out to the stairwell, asking Tati, "Is everything okay? What happened?"

"It is all good—great, actually!" Tati responded. "We had a girl baby!"

"Oh! Mazel tov, mazel tov! May you have plenty of *Yiddishe nachas*!" she responded joyfully, using a traditional Yiddish blessing that roughly means "May you get a lot of Jewish pride and joy from your child."

After all the mazel tovs had been exchanged, Mema Chaya turned to me with a sparkle in her eye.

"*You*," Mema Chaya said, "you could have told me there was *good* news! You had me so worried!" But she wasn't really angry, and we all laughed. Mema Chaya loved us.

And so, of course, when Tati decided he wanted me to change yeshivas in the middle of the year, he knew that Mema Chaya could make that happen.

She told the administration to accept me, and I was in.

But that didn't mean my troubles would end.

11

HEAVENLY BODIES

TWO DAYS AFTER Passover, I met my future principal. It was about two years before the day when Reb Yakovovitz and Tati and I had that discussion about my future.

The entire Stein family—Zeide and his brothers, Tati and his siblings, and many of our cousins—had gathered for a meal in honor of the previous rabbinic leader of the Tzhelim Yeshiva. It was the anniversary of his death, and the meal was an annual celebration of his life and influence.

Toward the end of the evening, Tati introduced me to a thirty-something-year-old man with a dark beard that appeared to have a mind of its own.

"Reb Chaim Shia Rubin will be your principal at Tzhelim next semester," Tati said. "And he is our cousin!"

We were only something like fourth or fifth cousins, but I guess Tati thought that if I knew we were related, I would at least try to behave.

I saw right away that Reb Chaim Shia was a real hothead. While his family mostly belonged to the Bobov sect, where he and I shared an uncle—the Bobov'er Rebbe—he had mostly attached himself to the ideology and teachings of the Satmar sect. He was a strange mix of a Hasid—he was a radical believer even by devout standards, and at the same time he did his own thing in his religious practices and his educational approach. He was all over the place, and not just intellectually. His black beard was always askew, and while his clothes were clean, they always seemed messy and barely put together. More to the point, he had an unpredictable temperament; one minute he'd be calm and relaxed, and the next he'd be irate, screaming in front of a roomful of students in the study hall over something that irked him.

Tati agreed that he had an erratic way of leading the school.

"I mean, really, can't you find someone better to be principal?" he asked Mema Chaya a few weeks after I started school. "Sure, the students kind of like him, but he is just too unpredictable."

"He gets the job done," Mema Chaya responded, in a tone that made it clear that she was not entirely convinced of her own words. Sure, it's not easy to keep a school of fourteen- to sixteen-year-old teenagers under control, but his manner of "getting the job done" was an irrational one.

When I started school, I decided I would try to be a good student and stay on the good side of the faculty. Once I took in Chaim Shia's personality, I knew I had to find a way into his good graces, and at first, I was successful. Within the first few days of the semester I learned that talking about our shared family heritage was one of his favorite pastimes, so I went with that. First I asked him what his favorite book about our family history was, and then I got him to share family stories and writings, even unpublished material he had collected.

Within a few weeks, I was going in and out of the principal's office several times a day, and for a change, it was not because I was getting into trouble.

Meanwhile, I was settling in nicely with the rest of the school, too. I loved my new teachers, the new environment, the diversity of sects, and the different Hasidic philosophies among the students. I also loved the yeshiva library, which was bigger than the one at the Shopron Yeshiva and had a better selection of books. It had all the books by the Viznitz'er Rebbes, as well as books that contradicted the Satmar sect's philosophies on Israel and other topics.

By throwing myself into my new surroundings, for a few weeks I was able to keep my gender identity and the religious questioning that came with it at bay. I focused on my studies, and I decided that I'd finish learning all the laws of Shabbos. I'd take the necessary exams on that portion of my studies to get one step closer to my rabbinical degree.

This worked for a while. But as I had learned before, I couldn't run from myself.

The trouble began a few weeks after I started school, when I decided to take my religious questioning to a whole new level by studying books I wasn't supposed to study. In the Hasidic community, that was quite easy, as the list of books that teenage boys are not supposed to read is quite long. These aren't just the regular forbidden books—books that were considered heretical—but also books that we were discouraged from studying too closely for a variety of reasons.

My great-uncle, the *Skver'er Feter*, used to say, "Do not ask which books we cannot read, ask which books we *can* read."

I didn't ask, I just read. First I chose a book that wasn't actually forbidden—in fact, the yeshiva library had many copies of it—but we had been told it was for reference only, and not to be studied in depth.

It was the Book of Joshua, the first of the biblical Books of the Prophets. The Book of Joshua, like the whole Hebrew Bible, is considered holy scripture and the indisputable word of God, but the students were discouraged from reading too much of it. We were never given a clear explanation, only that some stories "could easily be misinterpreted."

I quickly learned why.

I began the book and soon lost myself in the text. A few chapters in, I reached the part of the famous story where Joshua stops the sun—with God's help, of course—and the Israelites win a war against the Canaanites. They had to vanquish the enemy before the sun set and Shabbos began, so Joshua stopped the sun in the middle of the sky on a Friday until the killing was finished. It's an interesting story, and whether it's taken at face value or as legend, it shows both the love of God for his "chosen people" and God's supreme control over every aspect of the world.

So far, nothing was alarming. Then I read commentaries on the story, which included the writings of a thirteenth-century rabbi named Gersonides, whose work is controversial. While there are many canonized Jewish philosophical writings that are even considered sacred in the Hasidic community, studying them as a teenager is unacceptable—especially Gersonides, whose beliefs about God, faith, and the world to come could be considered straight-up heresy. In his writings, I read for the first time about different theological approaches to God.

In short, Gersonides suggested that—*gasp*—God isn't omniscient, an idea that goes against the central principles of our faith. He also seemed to believe that miracles don't exist in our day-to-day lives, instead citing an idea similar to what is called, in modern philosophical terms, "the Watchmaker God": a God who created the world but rarely intervenes in its daily activities.

As I delved into the teachings of Gersonides on Joshua, I read: "There was no such miracle that the movement of the sun and moon stopped as we mentioned because it's not true that a miracle can be introduced to nullify them [the natural movement of the sun and the moon]. It's impossible that such a miracle can happen in the heavenly bodies."

From there, he explained how, besides Moses, with no other person and in no other situation did God do anything out of the natural order of the world. No miracles, no "divine intervention."

In my mind, that meant that praying for anything was a waste of time. If something occurs naturally, then it will happen; otherwise it's tough luck. God isn't going to change anything just because you prayed for it.

As I reached this part of the book I was sitting in an empty study hall during lunch hour, not far from the open windows. It was a nice spring day, and I could smell the fresh leaves growing on the trees outside. Every few minutes I heard a train run down Broadway, just around the corner.

My brain froze.

Hold on, hold on, I thought. *So all these stories of miracles I have been told my whole life are what—fake? My entire life I was led to believe that there is one Torah, one God, and one way to interpret God's word. But here is a Jewish scholar who says it's not true, and that what I've been told my entire life is wrong!*

My head was spinning.

So much of my Hasidic education had been based on the miraculous stories performed by Hasidic rebbes throughout history. There is a Hasidic term that is used to describe any story that tells of a rebbe performing an open miracle: it is called "a Baal Shem'sker story." It is a reference to the never-ending well of stories about supernatural acts done by and for my direct ancestor, the Baal Shem Tov, the founder of Hasidic Judaism.

Believing in miracles was a key part of my belief system, and something that kept me at least a little bit grounded while I was questioning my beliefs.

"Someone who believes every story about miracles performed by the Baal Shem Tov and other Hasidic rebbes is foolish. But someone who does not believe any of the stories is a heretic. You have to believe that they could do it!" goes the Hasidic saying.

I had lost my blind faith long ago, when I had realized that the same people who swore that I was a boy also preached blind faith. Faith is beautiful for those who possess it, but I'd lost it at age twelve and never got it back. Believing in the divinity of our masters is what kept me going.

Once that was gone, too, I lost another ring in the chain that kept me tied to religious beliefs. But how was I supposed to believe in rabbis showing divine intervention when one of our own established scholars—and later, I learned that he was not alone in his assertions—claimed that even the prophets, even the biblical stories, are all merely inspirational, and not evidence of direct divine intervention really taking place?

One winter evening, years later in 2013, after I had already stopped being observant and joined Footsteps (the lifesaving nonprofit that helps people leaving Ultra-Orthodoxy, and whom I have to thank for my whole life outside of the Hasidic world), I sat in the house of a Hasidic philosopher and spoke about my religious disbelief. Reb Yitzchak Katz was someone who could

think on his own, up to a point—he never questioned the existence of God, the divinity of the Torah, or the divine authority
of the rabbis. Tati had sent me to talk to him after hearing me
announce—a few months earlier—that I no longer believed.

"You are a direct descendent of so many Hasidic rebbes," he
told me. "So you think all the stories that show that the rebbes were divinely ordained, that they possessed a holy spirit and
could change the natural order of the world, are just made up?"

"Well, yes!" I told him. I pulled out my phone, navigated to
the same Gersonides text I'd read in the library, and started to
read. When I finished, I looked up at Reb Yitzchak.

"Am I supposed to believe you over a thirteenth-century
scholar who was a more learned philosopher than you?" I asked
him.

He went quiet for a minute, and then he said, "Okay, fine. If
you don't want to be Jewish, why don't you go over to the priest
and convert to Christianity? Ha? You wouldn't do that, would
you? Because even you know that Judaism is right!" There was a
smirk on his face that said, *I got you.*

That's when I knew our friendship was over. Was he really
still living in sixteenth-century Europe, where the only alternative to Ultra-Orthodox Judaism was Christianity?

I had just told him I didn't believe in the Old Testament's
divinity, so what in the world made him think I would suddenly
believe in the divinity of both the Old and the New?

I shook my head, and soon after went home.

AFTER I FIRST read Gersonides, once again I felt alone with the
thoughts and ideas I couldn't share with anyone. It wasn't just
the words of Gersonides that shattered my mind—it was the

way he viewed the world. Putting aside the Book of Joshua and the stopping of the sun, Gersonides's idea that the natural world superseded all shook my own worldview. In the same way that someone questioning faith might learn of scientific principles that support atheism, I had a new set of beliefs to fuel my inner argument.

One thing was for sure: I was done listening to anyone who told me what I had to believe, and what I could or couldn't think.

Or read.

From there it was a slippery slope. I walked into a Judaica store in Williamsburg that sold all kinds of philosophical books, including controversial ones, and bought another Gersonides book, *The Wars of God*, a philosophical polemic in which he mostly disagrees with Maimonides and other canonized Jewish philosophers.

I didn't stop there. One book led to the next, and to more after that, until I eventually came upon two books that became my favorites: Richard Dawkins's *The God Delusion* and Richard Elliott Friedman's *Who Wrote the Bible?* I couldn't read English yet, so I read them in their Hebrew translations, finishing them in under a week.

It would now be close to impossible for me to go back and believe in a system that refused to indulge any of my questions.

Finally, I thought. *I know what's really bothering me. It's not gender, it's religion.*

IT WAS GETTING harder and harder to stay in yeshiva as a nonbeliever.

On the one hand, I wanted to succeed in a world that was the only one I'd ever known. I wanted to excel at yeshiva and become a rabbi. There was no other way of life that was even in my periphery. So I tried to suppress my religious misgivings, to quash my doubts and disbeliefs, even when I knew they were right.

On the other hand, it was hard to ignore them.

Am I the only mad person in the room who thinks prayer is a waste? I would think during prayer time. *Who thinks that there is no God?* I would wonder as we studied. The school was filled with students who questioned little and seemed entirely content with our way of life. And then there was me, questioning everything we were all supposed to believe and twisting myself up into knots.

There were days when I immersed myself in learning and thrived on our religious practices. I even went above and beyond, taking the stance of a zealot and arguing with everyone—Tati and Mommy included—that we should be even more observant.

Then there were days when I couldn't pray at all because I doubted God's existence.

All of this, coupled with my hot teenage temper and my feelings of being a girl, triggered a terrible depression. From the darkest places I would lash out. My teachers gave up on trying to control me. First it was Reb Chaim Shia, who told Tati that I was a "living orphan." Then it was Reb Skula, another one of my tenth-grade teachers, a loving man in his early forties with a long red beard and soothing voice. He tried to have an open and deep conversation with me to get to the "root" of my problems. While he was nice, he had no success.

At the end of my first semester, the administration was finally fed up with Reb Chaim Shia's temperamental ways. A new principal, Kalmen Halberstam, came onboard. Kalmen was even younger than Reb Chaim Shia, and also came from a rabbinic family. In fact, he was an even closer cousin: his mother was

Bobbe Meisels' first cousin. He seemed to like me, and we had a lot to talk about, from our families to my education.

Kalmen considered himself to be open-minded and philosophical.

"You are full of teenage zealotry, and I think that's great," he told me once. "It will help push you toward the truth!" He showed me books "proving" that evolution was wrong from a scientific point of view—and they might have worked to sway me had I not been well read on the topic from outside books.

Eventually, even he gave up. "I am afraid of the kind of questions your child has, and the kind of thoughts he plants in other students' minds," he told Tati.

Enter Reb Yakovovitz, who was sure he could convince Tati there was something wrong with me, and that together they could set me straight.

"My son is a seeker," Tati told him. "Perhaps the problem is not his but rather the lack of educators to address his concerns."

I'm not sure if Tati really believed that. Perhaps he knew there was something more existential behind my transgressions but wanted to protect me, so he did what he could. Either way, Kalmen was not pleased. He wanted me gone.

One day, toward the end of the semester in the winter of 5768 (2008), as I was finishing the first semester of twelfth grade, there was an uproar in the school—a moment of chaos that I didn't witness. I still don't know the full nature of what happened. But a student created an eruption, and when he was questioned, he blamed it on me. I was an easy scapegoat; I loved to cause trouble from time to time. But this time, I had no idea what had even taken place.

I was in the dining hall that afternoon when Kalmen came in, clearly angry, and pulled me from my chair.

"Get your belongings and go home. I am done with you!" he said.

"What did I do?" I protested.

"You know what you did, and I am not going to glorify it by repeating it to you," he said.

I hated when educators played the "you know what you did" game. Instead of going to collect my things, I ignored him.

After lunch hour was over, we all went into study hall to pray the afternoon prayers. I went, too.

I could see Kalmen's face when he saw me praying as though nothing had happened. He was not one for direct confrontation, but it looked like he was about to explode. Instead, he left and called Tati.

A few minutes later, a student came to tell me that my father was on the phone.

I went to the office and picked up the receiver.

"Come home right now!" Tati yelled.

"But I didn't do anything!" I argued.

"Well, come home anyway, and we will discuss it here," he said.

Fine. I would go home, but not before I made a stop.

I walked over to Kalmen's office and found him there talking to a few students.

I started to shout at him, saying, "I am going home now, but I want you to know this: I am innocent!"

He remained calm and pretended to listen to me, which only angered me more.

I went on, flipping the script on him and invoking God.

"I know you are picking on me," I continued, "and so does God. I will pray every day that the Divine punishes you. You will not get away with this!" I screamed.

Kalmen barely reacted. He just nodded his head and said, "Yeah, yeah, yeah. Get out of here."

I left his office, but on the way out, I opened the door all the way and knocked it shut with all the power I had. A booming sound reverberated through the whole building, a kind of "F you" that spoke louder than words.

Now he lost it. He stood up and ran after me.

In the main lobby, Kalmen caught up.

"You crossed a line now!" he bellowed, and I'm sure the entire study hall, perhaps the entire yeshiva, heard him.

I yelled back with every ounce of my energy.

"You are *rusha merusha*," I shouted, using the Hebrew term for "evil and wicked." "Know that I will never forgive you, never. Know that God will punish you for tormenting me. Know that you will burn in hell for eternity for what you are doing to me."

I was so hurt and angry that part of me actually believed what I was saying.

The yeshiva was listening, and Kalmen was growing paler by the minute. I could tell that, for a moment, he was questioning his own judgment. I went on.

"Know that there is a God in the world, there is a God in the world, and He knows what you have done!" I cried out. And then I left.

At home, Tati and I enacted a repeat of the scene of two years before.

"I still remember how you screamed at Reb Shimon that he was crazy," Tati yelled at me. "What in the world is wrong with you?"

This time, though, I refused to cave. I didn't cry or beg forgiveness.

Tati slapped me, twice.

And my two years at Tzhelim Yeshiva came to an end.

12

WELCOME TO THE CATSKILL MOUNTAINS

"**I WANT TO COME** join you for matzah baking today," I told my father on the way home from the mikvah on Passover Eve 5768 (2008). It was a nice, sunny day.

"Not this year," Tati replied. "I don't want you to come. I can't stop thinking about what you did, and I don't even know where you will be able to study next semester!"

That news fell on me like a bomb. I had convinced myself that Mema Chaya would be able to keep me in Tzhelim Yeshiva, but now I understood that I'd been wrong. I couldn't blame Tati for being angry and frustrated.

Still, to leave me out of matzah baking? Every year, at noon on the day before Passover, my father, like most self-respecting Hasidic men, went to bake matzah, the traditional Passover bread. It was one of my favorite holiday customs. Everyone dressed in their holiday clothes—though not their very finest, as those were kept clean for the big meal to take place that night. Baking matzah just a few hours before we were about to sit down to the biggest dinner of the year was supposed to be a reminder of the sacrifice of the Pascal lamb that was celebrated in Jerusalem on this day, at this hour, two thousand years ago in the times of the Temple. Singing psalms, the same way our ancestors did in the Holy Land, we kneaded the dough, flattened the bread, and rushed it into the oven before it could rise. God forbid if the dough entered the oven more than eighteen minutes after the flour first touched the water to make the dough: if that happened, it would be deemed unusable, a waste.

I loved the mix of holiday cheer, the smell of freshly baked matzah, and rushing, sweaty old men; it was one of my favorite moments of the year. I hadn't missed a single baking since I'd turned ten. It wasn't just fun, it was holy—making the matzah was in remembrance of a world that was gone, but it was also the ultimate preparation for the future. The heartfelt belief of every Hasid was that soon we would be back in Jerusalem to rebuild the Third Temple, once again sacrificing the Pascal lamb.

This year, I was cast out. Not only had I been expelled from school, but my future—the material one and the spiritual one—was in jeopardy.

ON THE THIRD day of Passover, as in every other year, all the men in my family—Zeide Stein, Tati, my uncles and cousins—headed to Monsey in Rockland County, New York, to celebrate the holiday with our cousin and holy leader, the Rebbe. The Rebbe was the eighty-five-year-old leader of the Viznitz Hasidic community of Monsey, and revered by all.

The Rebbe always welcomed us in a manner that was reserved for our family alone. After all, my grandfather, Zeide Stein, was the son of the Rebbe's "soul friend," his childhood friend from his old home in Eastern Europe. Additionally, the Stein family is one of the few families that has been part of the Viznitz Hasidic sect from the very beginning, going back to my grandfather's great-grandfather, who followed the first rebbe of the Viznitz dynasty, a friend and student of the Baal Shem Tov. The cherry on the top was the family relationship: my great-grandmother was a Twersky, a close relative of the Rebbe's mother, and a first cousin of the Rebbe's late wife.

Toward the end of the Rebbe's gathering, I realized that my father was quietly consulting with the Rebbe's second son, his "right-hand man," so to speak, and the head of the Gibbers Yeshiva, our community's flagship institution, located in the Catskill Mountains.

I walked closer to listen in, and my father beckoned to me to join the conversation.

"I am talking with the *Rav* here about getting you into Gibbers for the next semester," he said. "The Rav" was Rabbi Yisroel Hager, the Rebbe's son, who served as his second-in-command. We called him by his Yiddish nickname, Srulik. Srulik was also related to us in several ways, both through his parents and through his wife. After the Rebbe's passing in 2018, he took his father's place as Rebbe in Monsey.

Ah, so that's what the conferring was about. I listened in with a conflicted mind. On the one hand, going to Gibbers was the dream of many teenage boys of the Viznitz community. It meant finally being around hundreds of students who were all devout followers of *our* Rebbe. It also meant boarding in the Catskills, far from home, where I might have more freedom to read some of the books I'd recently discovered, books of philosophy that were forbidden. And it would mean that finally I would be a real Viznitzer without the mixed-in influences of the other sects that were the majority back home in Williamsburg.

However, it also meant changing schools in the middle of the year. It is a commonly held belief that there is something fishy about a student who switches schools for the summer semester. Changes were more common in the fall; in the summer, new arrivals were seen as questionable. And the question was, *What is wrong with you that you are coming here now?*

I worried that for the rest of my life, I would be *that* student, the one who was expelled from school at age sixteen—and not just any school, but a school run by my own uncle. Ultimately, though, I had no choice. There was no alternative. If Gibbers would accept me, I would go.

I have no idea what Tati told Srulik about why I was being moved. I am sure Srulik raised an eyebrow at the fact that Tati wanted me to switch schools in the middle of the year. But whatever that said to him about me, our family relationship out-weighed it. He arranged a meeting for me with Reb Yossel, the head adviser at the school, who was the acting dean on the campus grounds up in the Catskills.

"Okay, listen," Tati told me that night as we returned home. "You are going to go back to Monsey tomorrow morning. You can do the morning prayers with the Rebbe, and then you are going to meet with Reb Yossel in his home, just one block from the main synagogue."

So, at around noon the next day, I stood at the door of Reb Yossel's two-story suburban home. I was about to knock on the door when a horrible thought ran through my mind: *If I go to a school in the Catskills, I will be surrounded all day, every day, by hundreds of boys—just boys. I don't get along with boys. After all, I am a girl, and nothing will change that. In the city I can still get by, but in the woods? How am I going to survive that?*

I panicked. I had to get out of this. And I saw only one solution. In most yeshivas, the way to determine if a student is a good fit is with an oral exam, a Hasidic form of the SAT. I was sure this time it would be the same—and that I would have to flunk the exam. I would make sure to fail, and Tati would have no choice but to find me another school, preferably one in the city.

I knocked on the door.

A middle-aged man with a long gray beard appeared.

"A *gitten moed*—happy holidays!" he exclaimed, in what I suspected was amped-up enthusiasm. "You must be the Stein teen! The Rav told me all about you! It's an honor to meet Reb Yisroel Avrom Stein's grandchild," he said, mentioning my great-grandfather's name, a beloved figure to the older generation of Viznitz Hasidim.

We entered his *seforim shteeb*, a typical office for a Hasidic religious professional. The walls were lined with bookcases prominently displaying religious texts, probably including every single book ever published by a Viznitz Hasidic leader.

We sat down at a table, and he asked me if my family drank club soda on Passover. We didn't, as it wasn't considered homemade, a restriction of the holiday. He nodded and gave me flat water instead.

Then he began his interview.

"What do you expect to gain by studying in the Rebbe's Holy Yeshiva?" Reb Yossel asked.

"Well, my father thinks I am not doing well at my current school in the city, so he thinks Gibbers will be better," I responded, making it clear that I was not an ideal student, and that I was only meeting with him because my father wanted me to.

Reb Yossel smiled. "Sometimes, students who are not happy at the place they are studying find not-so-holy ways of expressing that. The Talmud says that a person is obligated to study at the place his heart tells him to. Our rabbis also say that 'changing a place changes your luck.' I think that's what you need. After all, you are a descendent of holy rabbis. Their merit will certainly help you!"

It was a very nice thought, but not at all what a scoundrel student expects to hear from an elder. Suddenly it dawned on me that this was all a formality. He wasn't going to examine me; my admission was already secure, and there was little I could say or do to change that. Either he didn't care how much I had learned, or even what I had done in my previous yeshiva to be kicked out, or he really believed that attending his school in the Catskills would help me. Whatever the case, whether he wanted me there or not, he had been given a direct message to enroll me—not just from the Rav, the dean of the school, but from the Rebbe himself.

If the Rebbe says do something, a devout follower doesn't ask why.

Our meeting soon ended, and I was on a bus back home. By the time I arrived that afternoon, my father had already received a call from the Rav confirming my admission to Gibbers.

The next two weeks flew by, and my father stopped being angry at me as his excitement grew. His enthusiasm was contagious, and I followed suit, hoping for the best. Once again, I convinced myself that if I did this—if I went to this yeshiva and did my best to conform—all these crazy thoughts that I was a girl would go away. After all, I had a strong mind, and I admired the Rebbe. *If the Rebbe says this is what's best for me, it has to be so,* I convinced myself. *Who knows? Maybe being around only boys for a while will show me how to be a "real boy."*

Still, before I finished packing, I made sure to sneak in *Who Wrote the Bible?* and *The God Delusion.* I was sure I would have no way to buy them in the Catskills.

YESHIVAT IMREI CHAIM Viznitz is its official name, or, as the devout followers of the Rebbe called it, "the Rebbe's school." Colloquially known as Gibbers, as it sits on Gibber Road in Kiamesha Lake, New York, it is the pride of the Viznitz-Monsey Hasidic community and the *liebling* of its late founder, the Viznitz'er Rebbe.

The campus, pleasantly rural, sits in the forest about five minutes off the main road that runs between Fallsburg and Monticello in the Catskills region of Sullivan County. The campus was originally built in the 1920s by the Gibber family, a secular Jewish family, to be a prominent Borscht Belt hotel where well-to-do Jewish families from New York would vacation in the summer. In the 1980s, as the Belt lost its prominence, the hotel was put up for sale. In 1990, after the Rebbe decided that Monsey was getting too urbanized to allow for undisturbed study, the Viznitz Yeshiva purchased the property, refurbished it, and turned it into a boarding school.

The yeshiva compound consisted of three main buildings: the study hall, the older dormitory, and the newer dormitory. The study hall was so large it could easily hold four hundred students. In the same building were several classrooms, a huge mikvah, some offices, and the Rebbe's room. The old dorm consisted of two floors above ground with the students' rooms as well as an additional half-below-ground-floor level that hosted study rooms and classrooms for the younger students, ages fourteen and fifteen. The new dorm building had an enormous dining hall that had been converted from an indoor pool, plus the kitchen, a laundry room, and three floors of dorm rooms, including what we called "the Senate"—the living quarters of the older students, age nineteen and up. All three buildings were connected by an indoor bridge so that students never had to go outside, something that was helpful during the harsh Catskill winters.

It was a relatively mild spring afternoon when I got off the bus after a two-hour ride from Williamsburg for my first day. It seemed as though it took barely a minute before I was pulling into the station and being approached by a young man in his early thirties. He introduced himself.

"*Shulem Aleichem!* My name is Chaim Meir Viznitzer, and I am the spiritual counselor for the first class. Welcome to Gibbers!"

I was one of four new students who would be joining the class of eighty in the summer semester, but Chaim Meir was told, as I eventually found out, to be on high alert for me and to watch me carefully. Reb Yossel later told him that I was "the student with one of the best brains on campus who likes to get into trouble and do his own thing every now and then." He followed that by quoting Reb Zalmen, my teacher during the morning session: "When the Stein student is engaged, the whole study hall can be in flames and it wouldn't faze him. But when Stein isn't in the mood, there is nothing you can do."

I think it's one of the best descriptions of my character I have ever heard.

A few hours later, after the other new students and I had a chance to settle into our rooms, we gathered in the study hall for Reb Yossel's welcome speech. It was actually quite informative.

"These are the yeshiva rules, as set by the Rebbe," Reb Yossel started. "Breaking these rules is disobeying the Rebbe's will." We exchanged looks; that was all the students needed to hear to know that we had to abide by the rules *or else*. Anything the Rebbe said carried almost the same power as a biblical commandment: going against the Rebbe wasn't just cause for expulsion, it was divine disobedience.

Then he outlined the rules.

"We have a border around campus and the map is posted on the wall. Going outside the border without permission is cause for expulsion. That includes going to the nearby village, even if it is only to go to the community's synagogue."

This didn't surprise me—wandering outside of the assigned campus borders was likely to be the strictest rule on campus. Not that there was much to do in the surrounding forest. The closest attraction was Kiamesha Lanes, a bowling alley located on Route 42, a twenty-minute walk from campus. There was also Anawana Lake, a typical Catskills lake with a few boat docks, a mere thirty minutes from the yeshiva on the other side of campus. Going to either of these places was strictly forbidden.

"Other dorms besides the one you live in are considered outside the border," he continued. "The same applies to another student's room and another student's bed. Two students are never to be locked in the same room alone. If two roommates are missing from the room, the other two students must sleep with the door propped open. If three are missing, the door can stay closed."

These were precepts I hadn't expected, and I found them odd. Later I learned they were put in place to combat the rise in homosexual activity, which was rampant in yeshiva, although I didn't know this at the time.

Then came the less urgent rules. "Going home from school is only allowed in one of the following instances: a sibling's wedding; an aunt, uncle, niece, or nephew's wedding; and for only one weekend either before or after the wedding. We ask that all the students schedule doctor's appointments during the time they are home during break; if it is an emergency, you can go home."

Other than the above, we were supposed to stay on campus for the whole five months of the semester.

With the housing sorted and the rules established, the semester went into full swing the next day. Our daily schedule began at 5:30 a.m., when we were awoken by the morning staff. We had half an hour to get dressed and head to the mikvah to shower and immerse ourselves in the ritual bath. We had to be in the study hall by 6:00 a.m.

At 8:00 a.m. we took a fifteen-minute break to get ready for morning prayers, which began at 8:15 sharp.

Breakfast was from 9:30 to 10:15. This was followed by the longest study session of the day, lasting until 2:00 p.m.

Lunch ran from 2:00 to 3:30, and during that time the dorms had to be quiet so that students who wanted to could nap.

Afternoon study time was from 3:30 to 7:00, followed by afternoon prayers.

From 7:30 to 8:15 we had dinner, and the evening study time, the most relaxed of the study times, then began. It lasted until 9:30.

This was followed by evening prayers, and then it was bedtime. Lights went out at 10:15.

The routine repeated itself five days a week.

The pattern to our days was both new and familiar to me. By the third day I was starting to relax and feeling more acclimated—I was learning the names of my teachers and classmates and settling into my studies as uneventfully as I could have hoped.

I especially liked the study hall, which was a good thing, considering the amount of time we spent inside of it. A short ramp led from the hallway into the study hall, bridging a two-foot height between the hallway and the large room. In the room itself, hundreds of students sat at wide tables. We all kept our textbooks open in front of us. Three of the walls were lined with bookcases, some stretching all the way to the ceiling, others tall and wide enough to obstruct the windows that circled the room. Windows that weren't blocked allowed the students a view of the surrounding forest. The fourth wall was home to a beautiful mahogany Holy Ark, which held the Torah scrolls. The Holy Ark was flanked by two small lecterns—one for whoever was leading the prayers and one for the Rebbe.

Also on that wall was a door, which led to my favorite room in the whole building: the library.

The study hall itself was filled with bookcases. These were for the basic texts—a Hasidic version of the classics, so to speak. There were biblical books, Talmudic books, books on the study of virtues, Kabbalistic books, books on Jewish law, and room for students to keep their private books. There were also thousands of Hasidic books. The first row was filled with the books of the Viznitz'er Rebbes throughout history; the second had the books of the Hasidic "founding fathers," the masters who lived and worked roughly in the eighteenth century, such as my ancestor the Baal Shem Tov, the Rebbe Elimelech of Lizhensk, the Maggid, and the Baal Ha'Tanya, the founder of the Chabad dynasty. There were rows upon rows, organized alphabetically by title, of books dating back to the 1700s.

Then there was the library, next to the study hall. It had the standard books you would expect every yeshiva to have—books that drilled deep into commentaries on the Talmud and Jewish law, reference books, Yiddish and Aramaic dictionaries, and so on. But there were also fun books. There were books on Jewish and Hasidic history, something that wasn't part of the education system in the Viznitz Yeshiva. My favorite sections, though, were the ones with books on philosophy and world history, all in Hebrew, of course. There were books that most yeshivas wouldn't have approved—the Gibbers library dated back to the founding of the yeshiva in Brooklyn back in the 1950s, when the censorship of books was more relaxed.

This was my version of heaven, my oasis in the forest. I spent time there studying the history of the world since creation 5,770 years before. I read about the Great Revolt against Rome in 66–70 CE, and the 150-year gap between the Talmudic timeline of the second half of the first millennium BCE and the timeline proposed by modern scholarship, which affects our understanding of the number of years the Second Temple stood. I read the details of the Crusades and about their cruelty, and about the pogroms against Jews in the years 5408–5409 (1648) of the

Jewish calendar. I might have known some of the details of all of that before, but now I read about them in depth.

ONE EVENING EARLY in the semester, I was sitting in my usual place at the northern end of the study hall, where the first-year students sat, when my gaze caught the sight of a student walking into the study hall.

He was a tall, skinny guy, with beautiful dark hair and light eyes. His clothes were neat and clean, and his posture and pace projected confidence.

I had noticed him before. He was a year older than me and very popular, but not the best when it came to studying, which is probably why I hadn't seen him in the study hall before. It was now the evening study session, when we had some freedom to study whatever we wanted, so I gathered my courage and walked over to him. His name was Chesky.

"Do you have a study partner?" I asked.

"Well, no, but I am not in the study hall most evenings," Chesky said, and I heard in his voice a sweet Canadian undertone. I didn't care if he studied at all, I just wanted to be his friend.

"Either way," I responded, "I just started studying *Mishna Berura*, on the laws of *Sefirah*. They are easy and fun. You should join me!" *Sefirah* is the seven-week period between the holidays of Passover and Shavuos.

"*You* want to study with *me*?" he asked, surprised. Apparently, I already had a reputation as a smart student, but I think that was based more on my rabbinic clothing than on other students actually knowing me.

"Well, I just got here, and it's not easy to find a study partner in the middle of the year," I replied.

"Okay, sure!" Chesky said. "Let's do this!"

I felt a strange tingle.

It was the beginning of a beautiful friendship. And so much more.

But that part would come later.

13

MATCHMAKING

"**I AM NOT SAYING** that people should dismiss the Hasidic dress code, there is value to it. It is just so sad, so wrong, and so misleading when it is such a big focus in today's Hasidic world!" Reb Yitzhak Moshe Erlanger said.

I agreed, but that wasn't my point.

"But my questions are not just about that," I responded. "I think being hyperfocused on materialistic religious garb and practices is just indicative of a bigger issue."

"And what would that be?" Reb Yitzhak Moshe asked.

"Well, I don't believe in the basics of our faith!" I dared to say.

Then I began shaking. It was the first time I had ever uttered those words to anyone; I hadn't expected to say them now. But since I had gone that far, I might as well keep going.

"I mean, is there really a God?" I continued. "No one talks about it—we just have to believe. Yet the more I study, the more I believe that religion is man-made. We can forget about proving

God's existence because it is quite obvious that religion is created by men."

"Interesting thought," Reb Yitzhak Moshe said. I was relieved, and bolstered. He wasn't angry! And for the first time in my life, I was talking to someone who took my philosophical questions seriously.

I took this as a sign that I could continue.

"And then the whole creation story—I mean, really? I will be honest with you, Rabbi, I have been reading up on evolution and science. Yes, I understand that we can't know what really happened that far back, but how am I supposed to believe that the world is only 5,769 years old?"

"Well, who said it was?" he asked.

"Who said? What do you mean?" I said.

"Well, from a Kabbalistic point of view, God has been building and destroying worlds for millions, or maybe even billions, of years," he said. "And given that so much of the mystic teachings are, well, mystic, we don't really know what that means."

"So, are you saying that the biblical creation story is at odds with Kabbalah? Are you saying the creation story is not real?" I said, both surprised and excited.

"The Torah not real? Heaven forbid! Everything in the Torah is reality, and facts from the living God. It is just that mysticism helps us to understand what it means. The Torah says that God created the world in six days, but the same Bible says that for God, a thousand years is merely a day, a metaphor," he said, referring to a passage in Psalm 90. "Ultimately, the Bible's story, and what you are reading from the wisdom of the gentiles, could actually align."

This was not what I ever expected to hear from a rabbi.

"I think you should study Kabbalah!" Reb Yitzhak Moshe exclaimed.

"But I thought you had to be older for that?!" I wondered aloud.

"Nah, not a Hasidic person!" he said. "You should go deeper into Kabbalah. I am sure it will help you!"

Little did he know how right he was, but for a very different reason.

IT WAS LATE on a Thursday night in Williamsburg, the one weekend of the semester that I was home, in the winter semester of 5769 (2009). I was sitting at a small, white marble kitchen table that was mounted to the wall in a basement apartment on Penn Street. Reb Yitzhak Moshe Erlanger was from Jerusalem, and this was where he was staying while in New York.

"You know," Tati had said when I arrived home from school, "Reb Yitzhak Moshe is here for Shabbos, and I got the number for his personal secretary. You should call him. Maybe you can get an appointment and meet with him." It was last minute, but I decided to try.

It had been a semester and a half since I'd started school at the Viznitz Yeshiva in Kiamesha Lake. Those first few weeks in the Catskills had gone very well. I liked the campus, I had some friends, and the rabbis were more engaging than any I'd met in my previous yeshivas.

"I don't even have to urge anyone to schmooze in the middle of study sessions!" I told Eliezer Yoel, one of my friends from Tzhelim, when he called me at school.

"Ha-ha, well, just wait a few weeks. We will talk then!" he replied.

Not having the urge to do anything but study is a rare experience, even for the most devoted yeshiva students. Everyone usually struggles to keep up with the study schedule. After all, it takes up eleven hours a day for weeks on end.

Not me. I was fully immersed.

In part, it was a survival technique. I knew that if I let myself have time to think, I would end up back where I was before, with an urge to act out, to question, and to run away. I would have time to indulge in impure thoughts about the fact that I was a girl. Immersing myself in study, in prayer, and in my new environment felt like the better option. I was finally making a few friends, boys at that, and I felt at home.

I was so immersed in yeshiva culture that I totally forgot about Hindy's engagement party, which was celebrated two weeks into the semester, in Brooklyn. A sibling's engagement was a family occasion that warranted a student leaving campus, and I'd been looking forward to it. Hindy had gotten engaged two weeks before, just a few days after the end of Passover. Given that I was "next in line" for marriage, and that I was close to both Tati and Hindy, I knew the details of her matchmaking before the engagement was made official.

"I am seriously considering that Weinberger boy, Reb Sholomo Leib's son," Tati told me during Passover. "He is a great student, he is close to getting his ordination, he comes from a nice and prestigious family, and I hear he is a really nice boy. This is exactly what Hindy needs."

I wasn't so sure. Reb Sholomo Leib was one of the four judges on the High Court of the Satmar community in Williamsburg. Prestigious, sure, but I still didn't like anything Satmar. Tati was right, though, and it was what Hindy wanted.

I had to think of another reason why it was not a good match.

"Reb Sholomo Leib is open-minded," Tati continued, seeing my hesitation. To be clear, he did not need my approval in any way, he just wanted to discuss it with me. "He even goes to the Rebbe sometimes!"

That was supposed to make me feel better. If Reb Sholomo Leib respected the Viznitz'er Rebbe, any doubts I had should have been assuaged. But I wasn't convinced.

"But a *Weinberger*, really?" I asked. "Would Zeide Meisels be okay with that?"

Tati blushed.

You see, most families in the Hasidic community had no issue with the Weinberger family, but some did. The Weinberger family, a four-hundred-year-old rabbinic dynasty, was tainted. I was fuzzy on the finer details of the problem, and in fact I am not sure anyone really knew them. If they did, they never spoke of it. But the gist of it was this: At some point in the nineteenth century, one of the ancestors of the Weinberger family had been a bastard, literally—a child born to a woman who had sexual relations outside of marriage. Once a bastard, always a bastard, says Talmudic law, and all of the bastard's descendants are forbidden from marrying kosher Jews. There was no way out of it.

Most families, and many rabbinic families, claimed that the Weinberger family rumor was false. In fact, Zeide Stein had married off three of his ten kids to descendants of the Weinberger family. Tati's brother David Shlomo married Mema Toby Horowitz, whose mother was a Weinberger. Then his sister Mema Tzirel married Yisroel Hager, the Rav's nephew, and his youngest brother, Feter Eluzer, married Fraidy Twersky, both children of Mema Toby's sisters.

Zeide Meisels, however, believed it. On the Meisels side of the family, out of the hundreds of marriages among the grand-kids of Zeide Meisels' father, there were less than a handful of them who had married Weinbergers. In a world where members of rabbinic dynasties all marry one another, it is not easy to avoid a whole clan, and the Weinbergers had married into many rab-binic families.

To me, this was just an excuse to avoid getting another Sat-mar brother-in-law. Faigy, my sister who had married just a few months before Hindy got engaged, married Mommy's first cousin, Lipa Teitelbaum, whose mother, Mema Rivky, was Zeide Meisels' sister. Lipa was a devout Bobov Hasid, even though his father was less attached to Bobov. Becoming a Bobov Hasid was a common occurrence on Mommy's side of the fam-ily, thanks to the familial connection to the Bobov royal family. I loved it. Yes, Bobov was still not Viznitz, but in a place like Williamsburg, where the majority was Satmar, everyone who was not Satmar was a breath of fresh air to me. I was hoping for another brother-in-law like Lipa.

"Yes, but it's not the problematic Weinberger," Tati said, ar-guing with me, "and Feter Mordechai Aron Meisels already ar-ranged a Weinberger match for his daughter. Zeide now knows that this part of the Weinberger family is okay." Feter Morde-chai Aron was one of Mommy's four brothers, and the one who was arguably the closest to Zeide Meisels. If he could do it, so could Tati.

"Are you sure about that?" I argued.

Later, Lipa came to my aid; I think he also felt we had enough Satmar in the family. "Why put a healthy head in a sick bed?" he argued. "Even if they are indeed not a problem, many people think they are, and when Hindy looks for matches for her kids, she will run into trouble."

Ultimately Tati asked the same person he always asked before agreeing to a match: the Rebbe. This time, he sent in his cousin, Chaim Meir Hager, one of the Rebbe's closest grandkids and confidants, to ask him about the match.

"The Rebbe says there is nothing to worry about," Tati told me the day after Passover. Of course the Rebbe said that. After all, his oldest son, Pinchas Shulem, was married to a member of the Weinberger family, Mema Toby Horowitz's sister.

The next day, Hindy got engaged to Avrom Shimon Weinberger, and the *vort*, a small celebration marking the engagement— not the main engagement party, which would be later—was held in our house. Only the immediate families from both sides attended, as was the custom. I met Avrom Shimon, and I actually liked him.

"Whenever we do something big at our rabbinical court, we think, 'What would the Viznitz'er Rebbe say?'" I remember Reb Sholomo Leib telling Tati at the *vort*. I liked that; it showed that at least he, and in turn his son, my future brother-in-law, respected the Rebbe and Viznitz.

We might just get along, I thought.

Hindy's engagement party was scheduled for two weeks later in Brooklyn. Up to that point, I had been to the engagement parties of all four of my married sisters, and I was planning to attend Hindy's as well. When I left home to return to the Catskills, I told my family I'd see them again very soon.

"Make sure you call us every day!" Mommy told me as I headed out. That was what my parents asked of all their children who did not live at home, even if we were just traveling. In a community where many people—including Mommy—did not even have cell phones that could send text messages, and where social media was all but nonexistent, phone calls were the only way to stay in touch. Mommy spoke to her mother, and Tati to both of his parents, every single day—other than Shabbos and holidays, of course, when the use of electricity is forbidden. Mommy spoke to her twin sister, Mema Zissi, every day, too. Most of the time while at Gibbers, I spoke to Tati and Mommy every day as well.

This was one of the most beautiful things about my family.

Until I got to yeshiva, I thought it was common practice among all Hasidic families. But just a few weeks after I started school there, Tati told me in casual conversation that his sister, Mema Tzirel Hager, and her husband, Feter Srulik, were on a trip to Israel. Their son Mendy was in my class in yeshiva, and I asked him why they were visiting Israel.

"Oh, they are?" Mendy responded. "I didn't know."

I was shocked. What did he mean, he didn't know?

"When did you speak to them last?" I asked him.

"Last week on Friday, before Shabbos," he said. It was now Wednesday, a whole five days later.

I didn't say anything, but I made it my mission to nonchalantly ask other students how often they spoke to their parents.

It turned out that about a third or so only spoke to their parents on Fridays, before Shabbos, to wish them a *Git Shabbos*, unless there was a specific reason to call in the middle of the week. Another group called home before and after Shabbos, and a small group of students called home three or four times a week.

I did not find a single other student who called home every day.

My parents were special, and I am forever grateful for that.

One Tuesday night, the second week of yeshiva, I called home after dinner just like always, but no one picked up the home phone.

I tried Mommy's cell phone, then Tati's, then the home phone again, and still no one picked up. *Interesting*, I thought. I wondered why everyone was out of the house and away from their phones, but couldn't come up with anything.

The next morning, I called home early. Mommy picked up.

"Is everything okay? Did something happen last night?" I asked. "I called all three numbers, but no one answered."

I heard Mommy's laugh over the line. "Ah, that is why you called us!" she said. "I was sure you knew—it was Hindy's engagement party!"

Oops! How did I miss that?

"We are so happy that you like it in yeshiva," Mommy said. "We didn't want to bother you."

At that time, just two weeks into the semester, I did indeed still like it.

14

TINGLING FEELINGS

"**HEY, DO YOU** want to go for a walk on the New Road after evening prayers?" I asked my new study partner, Chesky.

"Sure," he smiled.

Gibber Road—or the New Road, as we called it—had been built in 2003 as a way to keep traffic heading to a new community nearby from passing in front of the yeshiva campus. The yeshiva is situated on an older portion of Gibber Road, an L-shaped country road connecting to Route 42 on both ends, that had been renamed Yeshiva Drive. Since the old Gibber Road didn't lead anywhere else for the first twelve years of the yeshiva's existence, there had been no worry that the students would be disturbed by traffic or—*gasp*—women passing by. But then, when twenty-five families moved nearby to the new community, which was just north of the yeshiva, something had to be done.

So several actions were taken, and among these was the establishment of a five-hundred-foot buffer zone between the northernmost building in the yeshiva and the southernmost building in the village. Strict rules were enacted against yeshiva students wandering into the village without permission—even students whose families lived in the village were forbidden to leave campus.

And the New Road was built. But the New Road was fully within the permitted borders of campus. So, during lunch, and at night between evening prayers and curfew, many students walked along it as a way to refresh; this was actually encouraged by the yeshiva faculty as the only time for exercise.

"Are you sure you don't mind being seen with me?" Chesky joked that first night as we headed to the road.

"Nah, I like you. And I don't care what people think," I teased back. "And besides, the New Road is so dark, no one will be able to see us."

It was dark indeed. For the two weeks in the middle of the month when the moon was out, the night sky lit the road a bit, but when there was little or no moonlight, it was pitch dark.

Perfect.

That first walk turned into a second and then a third, and soon our walks became an almost nightly activity. We talked about everything. We talked about our families and our childhoods, and I told him about my rabbinic family and all that came with my lineage. We compared notes about which books we liked, which games we enjoyed, and which kinds of soaps we used.

Once a week or so I would walk with Mendy Hager, my only first cousin on campus, and every so often other friends would join us as well. But most nights it was just Chesky, me, and our growing feelings for each other. I knew I felt something new and different toward him, but it took me a few weeks to understand the nature of those feelings. Then it hit me. One day, I was studying the story of the illicit affair between King David and Bathsheba in the Book of Samuel when it suddenly dawned on me that I wanted to do with Chesky the same things that married people did.

At the time, I hadn't known that there could be an attraction between two people of the same sex. I only knew that a man and a woman got married and had a form of sexual relations. The mechanics of it were never discussed, let alone in the context of how it felt to be sexually aroused. I also had no awareness of same-sex attraction. But, of course, I was a girl, so it made sense to me that I was physically attracted to a boy, and my fondness for Chesky somehow seemed like further proof that I was a girl—because only a *girl* would want a *boy*, right?

As time passed, our nightly walks became longer and our conversations more intense. We never talked about our feelings, but it was clear to me that they were shared. We would intentionally bump into each other as we walked, and put our arms around each other—something considered taboo in yeshiva. We even allowed ourselves tight hugs when we parted. After we went to our separate rooms, my imagination would light up, thinking of all the ways I wanted to be a woman to him.

THEN SUMMER (OF 2008) arrived, the perfect time to spend outdoors in the lush green forests surrounding the yeshiva. Right next to campus, within the boundaries of where we were allowed to wander, there was a lake.

"Let's go out and study next to the lake," I said to Chesky one morning.

We headed over, taking our books with us. We both knew we were just going to talk the whole time, but we at least had to pretend that we were going to study, in case a faculty member questioned us on our way. We were allowed to study outdoors, although we weren't exactly encouraged to.

We got to the lake and walked around the edge for a while.

Suddenly I felt an intense urge to take Chesky's hand and hold it. I had never felt anything like it before, the pull to physically reach out, to touch. I wanted to hug him, tightly, too. I wanted it so badly I could hardly bear it.

"Why don't we sit down next to the old pool?" Chesky suggested. "I think there are some chairs out there."

Our campus had two overgrown outdoor pools from its hotel days. When the yeshiva took over, it didn't bother to fill them with water—some in the community considered it immodest for groups of teenage boys to swim together. One of the pools was right next to the dining hall, in public view. But the other one was a little farther away, hidden by an overgrowth of plants and trees that formed a natural wall around it.

We arrived and discovered there was only one chair.

"You sit in the chair," I said. "I'll sit on the ground."

Chesky sat in the chair, and I sat down close to him, sitting almost between his legs. I looked up at him and saw that he was blushing. My face felt hot as well.

Then we took each other's hands, and we talked about our feelings for each other. In a world where boys aren't encouraged to talk about their emotions, and in a community where expressions of love are rarely uttered, I had never felt closer to another person.

And for the first time in my life, I felt turned on, physically. I felt my pants getting wet. I put my hand on Chesky's lap, and there it was, the wetness, on him, too.

We awkwardly laughed at each other.

"Chesky," I said, breaking the silence, "you make me feel special. I feel as though my soul is connected with yours."

I think that would qualify as a Hasidic version of *I love you*. While Yiddish does have an expression for love, *Ich hub dir lieb*, I had never heard anyone say it, to me or to anyone else. Telling Chesky that my soul was connected to his was the only way I could think of to express my feelings.

"I feel the same way," he replied.

I stood up and kissed him on the cheek. Chesky's face turned redder.

"Is something wrong?" I asked.

"No, no, I like it!"

We looked into each other's eyes for a brief minute, and we both started blushing. I could feel an intensity building up in my body, a kind of heat I had never felt before. We smiled at each other and looked down at the grass. It was intense for both of us, and we needed a break.

And then we checked the time.

It was almost 2:00 p.m., time for lunch. We were expected to be in the dining hall.

"It's getting late," Chesky said, standing up quickly. "We better go."

On the short walk to the dining hall, we didn't say a word. Neither of us spoke, but we both knew that what we had just done was forbidden. The close hugging, holding hands, the kiss—these were all acts that we'd been warned to avoid since we were little. Staying pure and holy, and especially staying away from any actions remotely sexual, was the aim of every Hasidic teenager.

For the next few days, we avoided each other. But the next Saturday afternoon, on my way to my room after lunch, we ran into each other.

"Chesky, I want to talk with you," I said, my voice suddenly loud and tight.

"Sure, let's go on a walk," he said.

We walked.

"I know that what we are doing is not allowed," I told him. "But it feels right. I don't believe that sin can feel this good."

Part of me didn't believe my own words, but I wanted Chesky to believe them. And I don't know if he truly believed them either, but a few days later, we headed down to the lake again. There were a few boats in the water, and we took one and paddled to the middle of the lake.

That's where I kissed Chesky again.

This time, he kissed me back.

As his soft, strong lips touched my cheeks, I felt an electric pulse run through my body, awakening every nerve.

I kissed him back on the cheeks, and he kissed me again. And again. And then again.

After a little while, Chesky asked, "Do you like how my lips feel on your cheeks?"

"Yes," I stuttered.

"How do you think it would feel to kiss our lips together?" he asked.

"Well, the only way to know is to try!"

We locked lips.

I put my hands on his shoulders, and Chesky did the same with mine. We continued kissing and holding each other, pressing our bodies together. It felt like a combination of being on an intense roller coaster, with my heart jumping out of my stomach, and sitting on the most comfortable and relaxing couch in the world.

I'm not sure how long this lasted. I only know that we stopped when we heard the voices of other students approaching the lake.

I dropped my head into Chesky's lap and looked up at him.

"This feels so good," I told him.

He gazed down at me, his eyes alight.

"I will always like you," he said. "But we have to make sure we never tell anyone about this. These are our personal moments, and they are just for us."

FOR THE NEXT two months, we continued to take long walks and spend time at the lake; we would even sneak into closed rooms when we were sure no one would spot us. Our feelings vacillated between deep love and terrible guilt, and then back to telling each other, "This feels too good to be forbidden."

We both began to think we needed more privacy. We wanted to be able to do more.

"Did you know my father's camp is just down La Vista Drive?" I asked him one Thursday summer night as we were taking our walk, referring to a small country road.

"Yes, you went to visit your family there a few times," he replied.

"I did. My parents were there for nine weeks over the summer, along with the students from the school where my father teaches. But they're all home now, and the camp is empty, and I'm almost certain the pool is still full," I said.

"That sounds amazing!" he said. "We should sneak off campus tomorrow after the morning study schedule. No one will notice if we're missing on a Friday afternoon."

"Yeah, let's do it!" I responded. "Bring a bathing suit, it will be fun."

Chesky chuckled. "I don't have a bathing suit here. Why would I have one? It's not like *my* parents have a camp just down the road," he teased.

"Don't worry, I'm sure my parents will have an extra one in their bungalow. They leave their summer gear at the camp," I said.

We arrived at the back door to the study hall building, our favorite door to use after our nightly walks. It was a small double door right next to the mikvah, which was usually empty at night. It was 10:15, and we were less likely to be caught after curfew if we entered the building there.

"See you tomorrow after study session," we told each other as we snuck in a hug.

I woke up at 3:30 a.m. Friday morning, as I did every Friday morning, to get a few extra hours of studying in before Shabbos. This time, though, I woke with a strange feeling in my stomach, a feeling of desire that I couldn't explain.

At noon, the morning study session was over, and we were released to prepare for Shabbos. Instead of returning to my room, I walked down Yeshiva Drive to the "four corners," the intersection where the New Road intersected with an older portion of Gibber Road, Yeshiva Drive, and Gefen Lane, which led into the new community nearby.

Chesky was already there, waiting for me.

We headed toward Route 42.

Along the way we alternated between small talk and awkward silences, and after about fifteen minutes, we reached Lovers Lane—yes, that was really the name of it. It was a small road connecting Gibber Road to Route 42 on the right and La Vista Drive on the left. This was the part of the road still frequented by community members, and we could have been noticed, so we quickly turned left toward La Vista, and relative privacy.

I was experiencing feelings I had never felt before, physically and emotionally. I had felt the urge to hold his hand, to hug him, and to press my body close to his before, but never had I felt it in every part of my body like I did now. There were tingles in my stomach, and down below.

We locked arms and continued to walk in silence, but now it was an intimate one.

Twenty minutes later we arrived at camp. I went into my parents' bungalow and found him a swimsuit, and we walked up a short hill to the pool. The sun was out in full force. I could feel it on my forehead.

We entered the pool area and changed into our bathing suits. This time, the strict modesty laws of our community played in our favor, because the pool was surrounded by a twelve-foot green wall, so high that it was impossible to see in from the outside. The door had a lock from the inside, which had been installed to make sure that men couldn't see women swimming, and women couldn't see men swimming.

It was the perfect hideout for us.

We grabbed two pool chairs and lay down, the chairs touching.

"My mother took me swimming with her when I was two," I told him. "She put me in a floating tube and floated around in the water with me. It was one of the times when I really felt happy as a child! After I turned three, she didn't want to take me anymore, since I was only supposed to go swimming with the boys."

"Of course," he responded. "It is immodest for boys to swim with women."

We turned toward each other. Our hands interlocked. Our chests were naked, and we started to cuddle. As new as it was, I felt more comfortable with him at that moment than I had ever felt before.

"Yes, but sometimes," I dared to say, "I think that I am a girl."

The last time I had said those words aloud to another person had been to Mommy, when I was four, and it had left me traumatized. This time, I felt an intimacy that I had never experienced before, and that fueled my bravery.

He laughed it off with a gentle "Ha-ha. You do act girlish sometimes."

We continued to talk, and to cuddle closer and closer.

Finally, I leaned in and kissed him on the cheek.

He kissed me back.

We stopped talking and held each other, holding and caressing. It grew more intense by the minute. Neither one of us knew exactly what we were doing, but months of built-up feelings came rushing out, and we allowed them to.

We also both knew that what we were doing was wrong, and we couldn't face it, or each other. As we lay together, we pretended to be half asleep, even as we rubbed ourselves against each other, taking turns being on top and on the bottom.

Our swimsuits were slowly sliding down.

He was on top of me. We both moaned.

Soon I was fully naked.

Then our genitals touched.

We both gasped.

EVERY WEEK IN yeshiva, Reb Yossel taught a session on Hasidic teachings and light theology. He chose a different book of Hasidic classics for every age and would spend an hour one afternoon a week teaching it. It was also his time to cover any spiritual issues that needed extra attention, such as when the yeshiva bought a vending machine and students were protesting the concept of having access to food twenty-four hours a day. Having access to food at all times is considered by some to be a worldly materialistic concept to be shunned as too indulgent.

During the first month of the winter semester, at the beginning of my second term at yeshiva, he gave us a special talk. After half an hour of teaching a Hasidic text from the father of the Viznitz dynasty, one that addresses the importance of having a holy body and immersing in the mikvah, he closed the book, sat up straight, and went quiet for a minute. That was how we knew he was preparing to say something important.

"If you ever wake up, and you realize that you had a *mikrai lilah*," Reb Yossel started, "do not fall into despair." *Mikrai lilah* is the biblical term for a wet dream, something I'm sure very few students in the room, if any, had heard of before. Reb Yossel continued, regardless. "The first thing you have to do is to go to the mikvah as soon as possible. Even if it is Yom Kippur, the holiest day of the year, when you are not supposed to go, immerse in the holy waters. Then, as the Rebbe always says, reciting a few chapters of Psalms and studying a few pages of Talmud is all a teenager needs to fix that mistake."

The students, quiet in their confusion, waited for more.

"The most important thing," he finished, "is not to despair. Yes, it is a bad thing, but one of the foundations of Hasidic teachings is that despair is even worse!"

All one hundred students in the room went silent. I am quite sure that half of the class had no idea what he was talking about.

After a few minutes, Reb Yossel wrapped up. "If you need help understanding what I just said, or if you need help overcoming evil and impure thoughts, please come talk to me in private."

This conversation was the closest thing to sex education I'd ever had.

I was always warned against touching "down there," but that was all. Even the slightest mention of anything of a sexual nature was grounds for expulsion from school. Surely there were others like Chesky and me who had secret trysts—it was why we had such strict rules against being in a room with another student with the door closed. But the specifics were never spoken of. Or, if they were, not with me—I had a reputation as a devoted student and was known for my family, so it's likely that other students would keep quiet about such things in my presence.

One thing was clear, though—sex was not something anyone spoke about openly, ever. The Hasidic community goes to great lengths to avoid ever talking about sex, while making sure we all know that touching our private parts is a violation of our holiness code, the most despicable act of all. There was no "the birds and the bees" talk or anything similar. In fact, I was never told how babies are made and born, other than "an angel of God brings the baby to the hospital, and the Mommy goes to buy it there." I figured out on my own that babies come from a Mommy's belly when my youngest brother, Baruch, was born—but nobody ever told me, nor did I ask.

By the second grade, I knew my parents and teachers were hiding something from me. One day, before the remembrance day of Tisha B'av, one of the major fast days in Judaism (commemorating the destruction of the First and Second Temples), we were studying the five pleasurable things that are forbidden on that day: eating, drinking, washing, wearing shoes, and having sex. However, in class, my teacher translated the Hebrew term for having sex—*tashmish hamitah*, literally, "using the bed"—as "making the bed." We were told that on Tisha B'av, we were not permitted to make our beds after waking up, something that seemed like a nice reprieve to me. Then my cousin Moshe Meisels whispered in my ear, "That doesn't really mean making the bed. It's something married people do."

As the years passed, I picked up more hints and bits of information. In fourth grade, I read parts of a commentary on the Book of Leviticus that explained pregnancy, something we had skipped when we had studied the book in class. Then, in seventh grade, when our daily dose of Jewish law consisted of studying a nineteenth-century synopsis of the Orthodox code of law, I would secretly skip ahead to the section about the laws of purity. The teacher didn't bother to make sure we didn't read on our own, since most seventh graders weren't fluent enough in Hebrew yet, but I was. That's how I got a better sense of the biology of people who have menstrual periods, and how sexual relations generally worked.

I fantasized about having a period of my own.

The final details I learned from a booklet published for married men, which Tati had at home. The book included a warning in the opening pages that read, "This book is only for married people. For anyone who keeps this at home, please make sure to keep it in a secured place away from the reach of children. Be especially careful around young boys, as reading this booklet can give them impure thoughts and lead them to spill their seed in vain, heaven forbid."

Tati kept that blue-covered booklet hidden behind a row of books among his thousands of volumes of Jewish texts, but by the time I was twelve, I had seen every single book, this one included.

So there I was, in yeshiva, a sixteen-year-old teenager with the perfect knowledge of all the rules involving sex, but no information about how our bodies worked, and no way to understand that the physical feelings I was experiencing were caused by teenage hormones.

I may not have understood, but nothing—not even religious piety—can stop human nature from taking its course. Even when it's a girl who is mistaken for a boy, living on a sheltered campus with three hundred fellow teenagers.

AFTER OUR GENITALS touched, we both froze for a minute. Still pretending to be half asleep, we rubbed our bodies against each other.

Then, after a few minutes, I felt a hot spritz and heard a strong moan coming from Chesky. We both looked down.

"Oops! I'm not sure what this is!" he said. Neither was I.

"Let's just jump into the water and wash it off," I suggested.

We entered the water, and then we spent more time rubbing our bodies together. It was the most intense feeling I had ever had.

Over the next two years, until we both got engaged to other people, we explored each other in every way possible. We went from kissing and hugging to full sexual relations, just short of intercourse. We found creative places to express and fulfill our feelings, and while we had a sense that what we were doing was not in accordance with our community standards, we didn't stop. In truth, we weren't even entirely sure what we were doing. Only after we both got married, and learned about sex in Jewish law, did we realize that what we had done was similar to what married people did. I can't speak for Chesky, but to me, our connection made perfect sense. He was the boy, I was the girl, and we had sex outside of marriage.

Chesky was my first love, and I still feel emotional when I think of him.

15

AUDIENCE WITH THE REBBE

"WHAT KIND OF soap are you using?"

I was walking to the mikvah with Eliezer Duvid Schlager, a spiritual adviser who worked with the students. One of his jobs was to turn off the showers at precisely 6:00 a.m. There was only one place on campus where we could shower, and if we wanted to shower during the week, we had to make it to the mikvah before 6:00 a.m. Only on Fridays, in preparation for Shabbos, were the showers kept on during the day, until forty-five minutes before sunset. This meant that students might go days, even a week, without showering. I thought it was pretty gross for anyone to go so long without showering, but it was even worse for a bunch of teenagers going through puberty.

I showered every day. I didn't mind waking up early, and showering made me feel better. Somehow it made me feel a bit more feminine, more me.

"Um, I use Dove soap and Head & Shoulders shampoo," I told Eliezer Duvid, showing him the products I had in my hands.

"Really? This is what you are using?" he replied, seeming shocked. "They don't look or smell like something a Hasidic boy should use. Do you have to use a pink soap bar?" he asked.

I looked down at my soap. "This is what my mother gave me, and it's what we use at home," I replied, acting as though I'd never really noticed it before. In truth, I was very much aware that my soap could be considered feminine. But it was something I could get away with, even in an all-boys' school, and I didn't feel I needed to defend it.

"Are there any yeshiva rules against using specific soaps and shampoos?" I asked Eliezer Duvid, getting a little annoyed.

"Well, no," he said.

"Do you ask all the students which kind of soap they use?" I asked him next.

"No, I don't," he answered.

"What do you want from me, then?" I asked. He was making me uncomfortable and I wanted him to go away. I was trying to be a good student, but having an adviser smelling my business was not part of the deal.

"Well, I believe in you, you are a *rebbishe* child," he said. "I think you have great potential, so I am trying to look out for you, to help you. I also noticed that you shower every day, which is a very girlish thing to do."

Of course, I wanted to say, "Yes, I know, that is why I am doing it." But I couldn't, so instead I kept my retort simple. "I'm used to it. I've always showered every day."

Eliezer Duvid shook his head and moved on.

I didn't know where all of that had come from, but one thing was clear. I was under a magnifying glass, and I was not happy about it.

MY ALL-OUT CAMPAIGN to suppress my gender identity, and in turn my irreverence for religion and theology, lasted for just a few weeks. Five weeks into the spring 2008 semester, I was back to grappling with my identity. The only explanation I could think of that made any sense was that I was not fulfilling what I came to the world to do, and my thoughts that I was a girl were somehow tied to it.

I decided to ask the Rebbe about it.

As a relative of the Rebbe, it was fairly easy for me to get a private audience with him, even when there were thousands of people clamoring for his attention. So I made arrangements to spend the Shavuos holiday in Monsey, where he lived. I'd stay with Yakov Yosef Hager, the Rebbe's grandson, and his wife, Shifra, as I often had before. Yakov Yosef would eventually (in 2018, when the Rebbe passed away) become the Grand Rebbe of the Viznitz community in Borough Park, with a following of around ten thousand Hasidic people.

After evening prayers on the first night of Shavuos, I asked Yakov Yosef if it would be possible for me to ask the Rebbe something personal, alone.

"Of course," he said. "Tomorrow night we are having dinner with the Rebbe at his house. I'm sure you could to talk to him between prayers and the meal."

On Shabbos evenings and on the first night of every holiday, the Rebbe always had his meal in public, in front of thousands of Hasidim. The second night, the Rebbe ate at home, with family. We all loved that time with the Rebbe; it was one of the few times when our family had the Rebbe to ourselves. It was as if he were a king who would set aside his crown for a time to show that he was also a father and a grandfather.

After prayers that evening, I went to the Rebbe's house. It was large and beautiful, set on a hillside majestically overlooking the castle-like synagogue. The Rebbe had fallen in 2003 and stopped walking, so there was also a bridge connecting his house to the synagogue, and that somehow made it look even more royal.

At his house, I was welcomed inside, and after a few minutes, Yakov Yosef's brother, Chaim Meir, another one of the Rebbe's personal secretaries, came out of the Rebbe's study.

"My brother told me you wanted to talk to the Rebbe," he said. "Now is a good time! The Rebbe is studying before the meal, and he is in a relaxed mood. Go on in."

I went into the Rebbe's study. "*Git Yom Tov*," I said, introducing myself with my name. "I am Mendel Stein's child, and I am staying here for the holiday!"

The Rebbe nodded as soon as I mentioned Tati's name. He knew him well.

"*Git Yom Tov*," he said with a smile. "Are you enjoying your visit for the holiday? Where are you staying?"

"I am staying with Yakov Yosef, and everything is great. I'm very happy to be here," I assured him.

"So, you are eating with us today?" he asked, giving me a loving pat on the cheek, his usual sign of affection.

"Yes, but I also wanted to ask the Rebbe something personal," I said.

The Rebbe half closed the Talmud volume in front of him and turned to face me, fully listening.

I cleared my throat. "I am struggling a bit in yeshiva with what to study," I began. "I mean, there are so many options, so many areas to choose from. How can I know which path is right for my soul?"

The Rebbe looked surprised. A Hasidic master, he was rumored to have been a Kabbalistic scholar, but he rarely used any language of mysticism himself. He clearly was not expecting to hear a sixteen-year-old ask him questions about the soul.

After a minute of quiet contemplation, the Rebbe spoke. "The Zeide used to say"—the Zeide was his grandfather, Rebbe Yisroel Hager of Viznitz, who passed away in 1936—"the Zeide used to say on the matter of the soul, 'I am a specialist!' But he said that about himself, not about me. I do not understand people's inner souls. However, if you start by studying Talmud, I am sure that the light of the Torah will guide you to the right path."

This didn't really help me, but I didn't say anything more, other than to offer my thanks. I knew it was all he was going to offer. Studying Torah was his solution for many problems, like a nurse prescribing painkillers without looking for the root of the problem.

I was on my own again.

THE NEXT FEW months were a roller coaster of thoughts and feelings. I tried to immerse myself in studying, and instead found myself sick and depressed. I developed intense sinus problems, which I'd had before, but they strangely seemed to grow worse when I was especially unhappy. It was as though my body was responding to the trauma my brain was feeling by shutting down physically.

I developed a cycle that I repeated over and over.

First, I would try to immerse myself in studying. Then, my thoughts about being a girl would return, and I would turn to philosophical questioning, trying to convince myself that I was only having these thoughts because of my religious disconnect.

Then I would decide that I did not believe in any of the religious teachings at all, and my anxiety would surge, as I saw no way out.

After that I'd fall into depression—and develop a sinus infection. Having an infection meant I needed to see a doctor, which gave me the perfect excuse to leave campus and take a two-hour ride to Brooklyn. The doctor would confirm I had an infection, give me antibiotics, and tell me to rest for a day—the perfect excuse to stay home, in bed, where my depression wanted me to be anyway. I would take the antibiotics, and as soon as I started feeling better, I would go back to yeshiva refreshed. Then I'd attempt to immerse myself in studying all over again.

The cycle repeated as many as eight times, each cycle taking about two weeks.

In the middle of all this, I finished reading the forbidden books I snuck into yeshiva. My philosophical questions shifted from my discomfort with religion to evolution, creation, and the origins of the Bible and religion. I craved more words, more ideas. There was a student in yeshiva, Duvid Rubin, who had a connection with a Hebrew bookseller in the Catskills, and he said he could get me any book in Hebrew. I asked him for two more books by Richard Dawkins, *The Selfish Gene* and *The Blind Watchmaker*, which had both been translated from English in the 1990s. I finished both in a matter of weeks.

There was another book I read, too, this one from the yeshiva library. It was called *The Book of Knowledge* and had been written by an Ultra-Orthodox author who claimed to also be a scientist. He tried to show how science and Ultra-Orthodox beliefs went hand in hand. The book itself didn't interest me—only a small footnote within it did. It mentioned a former Israeli rabbi named Yaron Yadan, who had become an atheist. In the book, the author wrote that all of Yadan's arguments were wrong, and so were his commentaries on the authenticity of the Bible and Judaism.

I had never heard Yadan's name before, but I knew I wanted to read his writings. So I told Duvid Rubin I was looking for any books by Rabbi Yaron Yadan, an Israeli scholar of Jewish law. I also told him that because Yadan was not Hasidic, no one could know that I had asked him for it. I think Duvid appreciated a good rebellion when he saw it, so he agreed to keep it quiet.

A few weeks later, Duvid came over to my room one night just before lights out and handed me a bag. "Here is the book you wanted," he said. "At least I think it is." It was a book by Yadon that had been published just a few months earlier. Its Hebrew title translated roughly to *Religion Defies Its Creators*. The book dives into the depths of Judaism, showing how it is man-made, and how its teachings are backfiring against religious people.

It was the most intense, direct rebuke of Orthodox Judaism I had ever read. It was all I needed.

I am finished with Judaism! I decided.

Not that it was so easy to be finished. To not practice our way of life meant leaving it—I couldn't stay at yeshiva, or live in Williamsburg, and not follow the practices of our community. But leaving the community would be a radical move; whenever someone did that, which only happened rarely, it was widely demonized. The belief among Hasidic people was that to leave was to live one's life as a failure, a criminal, mentally ill.

But I knew it was possible. My cousin Luzer Twersky had left the community not long before, becoming the first person in my family to fully leave the Hasidic community. The family had been stunned, and we were told a load of stories about how damaged he was. I didn't care. I just had to figure out how I could get away, too. I would have to bide my time.

One day, in the beginning of the winter semester in 5769 (2009), as I was browsing the yeshiva library, I found a small book on the bottom shelf. It was simply named *Hassidism???*

The book was a stinging rebuke of modern Hasidic culture. It made fun of Hasidim who think that Hasidic Judaism is all about the clothes they wear, the specific songs they sing, and the laws they enforce. I could relate to it immediately. I finished the book and found three more by the same rabbi.

I read the three follow-up books. In one of them, called *Hassidism!!!*, the author goes into detail about what Hasidism is really about. He speaks of the beauty of the holidays, the importance of spirituality above the letter of the law, the purity of intentions, and the great value of happiness.

I loved it.

The author's name, Reb Yitzhak Moshe Erlanger, sounded familiar, and I remembered that Tati had his books at home.

"I just read four of Reb Yitzhak Moshe's books," I told Tati when I spoke with him next. "I really loved them! I really feel like he is speaking to me."

"Wonderful," Tati said, "I like his teachings, too! I have many of his books at home."

It was still not enough to keep me religious, but it was a start.

A FEW WEEKS later, it was time to go home for the semester's Shabbos visit. It just so happened that Reb Yitzhak Moshe would also be in Williamsburg that weekend, for his yearly visit to his followers in New York. Tati got his secretary's phone number.

I called the number, hoping to make an appointment, feeling not a little desperate. *If there is anyone who can save my Judaism, it is Reb Yitzhak Moshe*, I thought.

"Reb Yitzhak Moshe is busy today, and I doubt he will have time to see you. Maybe try again next week," his secretary said.

"But I study outside of the city, and this is my only chance!" I pleaded.

"Well, come by at ten o'clock after evening prayers, and you can talk to Reb Yitzhak Moshe when he eats dinner. You'll have half an hour," the secretary relented.

"I'll take what I can get! Thank you!"

I showed up. We talked.

First I shared my background a bit. He remembered Bobbe Stein's father, who was the Spinka Rebbe in Jerusalem. Soon, though, we were delving deeper into my questions. I told him I'd read his books, and about the impression they left on me, and the struggles I still had. I didn't tell him about my feelings of being a girl, of course, but I did say I felt untethered from my Judaism.

What was supposed to be a half-hour conversation lasted almost five hours. At 2:30 a.m., I finally left, with a clear message from Reb Yitzhak Moshe: "Dive into Kabbalistic studies. It will help you!"

I had nothing to lose.

Reb Yitzhak Moshe told me to start with two books in particular, both of them from the writings of Rabbi Chaim Vital, the sixteenth-century mystic who had written down the teachings of Rabbi Isaac Luria, known as "The Lion"—the father of modern Kabbalah. One was *The Treasures of Life*, an introduction to mysticism; the other was *The Door of Reincarnation*, a study of human souls and their place in the world.

The first book was helpful, even enlightening, but it didn't offer any real clarity about my own life. I opened the second book and began to read.

It was early on a Friday morning that winter when I reached Chapter 9. The chapter focuses on the gender of souls, and how different souls may enter different bodies throughout time.

I was sitting at my usual place, at the table mounted to the eastern wall of the study hall. There were only a few other students in the study hall at that hour, and the room was quiet. In front of me was my book on my bookstand, which I'd been reading in the dim light, drinking a cup of Taster's Choice as I turned the pages.

In Chapter 9, I read:

"At times, a male will reincarnate in the body of a female, and a female will be in a male body," the words jumping up from the page in front of me.

I froze. I read it again. And again. And again.

For the first time, after sixteen years, I had found a text that justified my existence. Maybe I wasn't crazy after all!

I stood up from my chair and left the study hall, walking outside into the cold air, into the forest, where I cried like a baby.

16

HIGH ON MYSTICISM

"**D**O YOU WANT me to tell everyone about how you fasted yester-day?" Eliezer Duvid Schlager half screamed at me.

A group of some twenty students had gathered around us with shocked expressions on their faces, witnessing my heated debate with the spiritual adviser. By this time Eliezer Duvid had also become a friend, and he was worried about me.

That didn't mean I appreciated his interceding.

"Or how about Monday, and last Monday and Thursday, and weeks before that?" he continued.

"So what? Yes, I fasted," I replied. "It's during these weeks that Kabbalah teaches us it is a time for repentance, the salvation of the soul, and the correction of impurities!"

"But you are a young teenager!" Eliezer Duvid responded. "It is not healthy for you to do this at such a young age!"

I began to tear up.

"Do you really have nothing better to do than to pick on me?" I said, crying. "I'm trying my best to become holier!"

"Yes, but did anyone tell you that *this* is the way to do it?"

"We all have to work on divine worship and connection in the way that works for us individually. So what if I go to great lengths to do that? Do you really want to be responsible for stopping me if this is indeed the right path?" I asked, raising my head in defiance.

Eliezer Duvid blushed. "I'm just doing what I think is best for you," he said.

"Well, I am not worried about myself, and you don't need to be either," I responded, this time facing the crowd that was still watching, stunned. "I can and will stand my ground, and do what is best for me and my Judaism!" I sobbed. "But I'm worried about all the people who are here listening to you. Because of you, some students may stop taking spiritual initiative. Who knows how many times you will prevent God's joy in people resulting from amazing spiritual deeds?"

In truth, I was standing up for myself more than expressing a concern about other students' spiritual paths. It was just my way of saving face and coming out on top in this ridiculous argument. But my point was sound.

Moishy, a student in the cluster around us, jumped in. "It's not like a teenager will gain anything from Kabbalah. It's a waste of his time," he said.

Now Eliezer Duvid came to my defense. "No, no, that's not what I am saying. Of course he is gaining a great deal from studying Kabbalah! He just has to be more careful in how he applies it!"

So Eliezer Duvid supported me, just within limits.

IN YESHIVA, FIRST-YEAR students were not given a choice of what to study during the morning study period. The only option first-year students had was to study the Talmud, the deep study way. After the first year, students were permitted to choose between studying Talmud and studying Jewish law, and I wanted to begin my Jewish law studies right away. Studying law, especially the laws of Shabbos and the laws of kosher food, would put a student on track to become a rabbi, but most students chose to study Talmud. It was the more prestigious, nobler selection.

"What if I don't want to focus so much of my time on deep Talmud study?" I pleaded with my first-year adviser, Chaim Meir Viznitzer.

"First-year students don't get a choice," he replied. "And besides, we, the school advisers, believe that a good student needs to master Talmud first. Later, after you're married, you can study law."

"That's just wrong," I responded. "I'll still be studying two pages of Talmud per week, with the medieval commentaries, which is where we actually gain Talmudic knowledge. In the morning session, we spend weeks on a single page, finding questions just so we can answer them, for the sake of 'dissecting the text.' It's a waste of time!"

"It's only through deep Talmud study that you can gain the skills you need to properly dissect the laws," Chaim Meir argued.

"You don't really believe that, do you?" I said in my old "gotcha" tone.

I had my reasons for arguing the point. I knew that one day soon I might have to leave the community, and I wanted to learn Jewish law before I did. If I was going to rebel, I wanted to know exactly what I was rebelling against. Getting ordained, and knowing all the Orthodox laws, and *then* leaving—that was an educated choice.

My need to rebel, to be different, was also triggered by my being a girl inside. Being different on the outside—not fitting in—felt right.

By now I could tell that Chaim Meir was irritated with me. It wasn't his fault. My resistance to deep study had percolated among the students and reached the administration, and they were worried. For years, the yeshiva administration had expected all "good" students to study Talmud even after the first year. At the time, there were only twenty students who had chosen the path of studying Jewish law, and to many in the leadership, it was a source of pride that the majority of students chose Talmud for their long-term learning. My rebellion against it was not to their liking. There I was, a "smart" student, advocating for another way.

What I couldn't understand was why the law cohort existed if the administration wanted students to study only Talmud. It wasn't like the yeshiva was known for offering choices anyway. Heck, we didn't even get to choose which kind of white shirt we wore. "Choice" was not on the menu for anything else—why offer this, only to discourage it?

Chaim Meir stood up from his seat, put his hand on my shoulder, and said, "Let's go on a walk and talk."

"Are you saying that you have made up your mind to study law next semester?" Chaim Meir asked me as we walked down the ramp out of the study hall.

"I sure have," I responded. "I want to become a rabbi, and I don't see any reason why I have to wait until I get married to start my studies."

Chaim Meir already knew that trying to get me to do something just to "fall in line" with everyone else was futile, so he took another route to dissuade me.

"Do you ever think it might hurt your chances of finding a good bride? After all, you are already sixteen, and you come from a rabbinic family, which means that matchmakers are already observing you. The students who study law are considered less intelligent. What message will that send to your bride's family?"

Now I was angry, and I raised my voice. "So let me get this straight. The yeshiva encourages all the good students to study Talmud, and as a result the students who choose law are labeled as below-average students. Then you use the reputation you created to deter other good students from joining? This is a vicious cycle!"

By now we had attracted the attention of a few students, who were listening in. Chaim Meir took my hand and led me out of the room.

"Okay, okay, I see your point," he said when we were outside. "But let's calm down and talk about it like adults. Can we do that?"

This was a new kind of reaction from a superior. I was used to my verbal outbursts ending conversations and leading to the superior giving in, or at least giving up. This was a welcome change.

I took a breath and lowered my voice.

"Then why do we even have a law program at yeshiva?" I asked him.

"I will tell you," he said, and he began to explain. "When the Rebbe opened the yeshiva in 1954, there was no deep study program, just like most Hasidic yeshivas in Europe. In the morning session, the Rebbe would teach Talmud, and in the afternoon, the entire yeshiva studied law. Then the administration wanted to hire Rabbi Shor and start a deep study program, which had become prestigious. The Rebbe agreed, but on three conditions: One, that we hire someone of Rabbi Shor's standing to teach an alternative to deep study for students who didn't want to immerse in Talmud. Two, that we continue to have a study session in which every student studied two pages of Talmud per week. Three, that every student be given a dedicated time to study some law."

I thought about that. The Rebbe, the spiritual supreme leader of our school, wanted us to learn law. I had the Rebbe on my side! I grabbed hold of that truth and repeated it every chance I got.

To the dismay of the yeshiva leadership, my argument spread. The next year, about fifty students joined the cohort studying law, the biggest cohort ever.

REB BERISH WAS the chair of the Jewish Law Department and one of my favorite teachers. A sweet middle-aged man, he was open-minded in a way that was unique in the Hasidic world. He was also an ordained rabbi, which meant that if I studied hard enough, he could eventually examine me on my learning and ordain me as a rabbi. Getting ordained was important to me for two reasons: it would give me solid work opportunities and prestige in the community, and, should I decide to leave the community, I would at least know the rules that I was rebelling against.

I also loved Reb Berish's approach to studying. Instead of delivering daily lectures, the way the Talmud teachers did, he gave us weekly handouts with lists of texts we were to read, complete with the sources we needed to study on our own. Every Monday, when the majority of students would be in their classrooms listening to two-hour lectures on deep Talmud study, we, the forty or fifty students studying law, would be in the study hall, reading and learning on our own. Reb Berish was there to help if we had a question, but most of the time we studied alone, at our own pace. Then, on Wednesdays, he would give one two-hour lecture recapping everything we had covered, to ensure we were on the right track and understood the lessons.

We started studying the laws of eating and mixing dairy and meat, arguably the most complex part of the kosher food laws. I was happy—not just because I could study law, but because I had changed, at least a bit, the environment at the school and the attitude toward studying law.

In the eyes of the school administration, that also codified me as a troublemaker. I became known as the "kosher rebel," the student who used religious, Hasidic-infused arguments to be rebellious.

Toward the end of my time in yeshiva, in the summer of 5770 (2010), however, my public study of law got another direct seal of approval, the highest seal of all: the Rebbe's.

During that time, I was at my peak of Kabbalistic devotion and studying on my own. It was almost an addiction. Studying filled my life to a point where I often followed my own schedule rather than the yeshiva's, in order to follow the teachings of Kabbalah. The window of time from sunset on Thursday night to Friday morning is considered one of the holiest times of the week in Jewish mysticism—and in Hasidic teachings, too, which helped me to not be a complete outsider. Called *Leil Shishi* in rabbinic Hebrew—literally, the night of the sixth day, though in modern Hebrew that term is used to refer to Friday nights rather than Thursday nights—it is a time when the gates of heaven and the gates of wisdom are wide open.

In yeshiva, we celebrated Leil Shishi in many ways. First, during the last forty-five minutes of the afternoon study session on Thursdays, we gathered together and sang songs of Shabbos, shared Hasidic teachings, and followed Hasidic meditations.

Then, before the evening prayers, we would sing the old European Shabbos folk song "Git Shabbos, Git Shabbos, Oy Vay Oy Vay." The song ends with the words "Shreit'she ala Git Shabbos"—"Let us all scream 'Good Shabbos'"—a way of demonstrating our readiness to welcome the next night.

But the most significant way of celebrating Leil Shishi came on Friday mornings, and it was optional. Waking up earlier than 5:30 to study during the week was technically allowed but strongly discouraged—even yeshiva students have to sleep some-times. On Friday mornings, however, waking up at 3:30 to begin studying at 4:00 a.m. was somewhat encouraged, and actually quite common. On an average Friday morning, by 5:30 there would be as many as a hundred students already in the study hall. Through my entire two and a half years at yeshiva, I could count on one hand how many Fridays I missed waking up at 3:30.

Kabbalah was a lifeline. I had found myself in a sixteenth-century text, and a new phase of my life had begun. I related to the teachings so intensely that it kind of gave me a high. Mysti-cism can be almost a psychological drug—at least it was for me. At the peak of my devotion, I would sit on the fields of the cam-pus, imagining God and the angels in nature, and seeing the life in plants and trees. I felt the soul of every blade of grass, and I would talk to the sky and feel its responses. It was like dreaming, but while still being awake. It left a lasting impact.

17

ENGAGED

"SO, HOW MANY siblings do you have?"

"I have nine—five brothers and four sisters," Fraidy said.

I already knew that, actually. This might have been my first conversation with Fraidy, but I knew her family well. Her older brother Srully was a friend from school, just one grade above me. Fraidy's maternal grandfather was Bobbe Stein's mother's first cousin, and Fraidy's mother's sister, Shifra, was married to Mommy's brother, Feter Duvid. All in all, we were related multiple times over, by blood and by marriage.

We were sitting across a dining room table in Fraidy's sister's apartment in the Borough Park neighborhood of Brooklyn. Our meeting had been arranged by a local matchmaker, and it was the first time either of us had been on a "date." Not that it was called that. It was called a *bashow*, a chaperoned get-to-know-you meeting with the stated purpose of deciding if we should marry—even though by the time many couples, us included, meet, it is already almost fully decided to move ahead with the engagement.

At first, we spoke of mundane topics, like summer camp and yeshiva. I told her about some of our family traditions, and she told me about her time visiting Israel as a young girl. I kept my head up but took care not to look directly into her eyes, as I had been instructed. Hasidic boys are always told not to stare at women.

"What am I supposed to say to her?" I had asked Mommy on our way to Borough Park.

"Oh, don't overthink it," Mommy said. "Just ask her about her family, ask her about her school, and so on. After all, this is the first girl you are talking to, so you are not expected to know how to keep up a conversation."

"Anyway, this is just a formality," Tati injected. "Trust us, she is the best girl for you. Just have a quick chat, and then tell us what you think!"

I was about to meet the person I was supposed to spend the rest of my life with, the person I was supposed to create a large family with. And Tati and Mommy were telling me to rely on them, and not worry about deciding on my own? Since when did I not have opinions of my own?

But I did want it to work out. I wanted to like her, and I wanted to get engaged. My whole life, I'd been told that the coming-of-age years are all preparation for marriage and adulthood, and I was eager to begin that phase of my life and put my childhood behind me. Nine other students in my grade at yeshiva were already engaged.

Besides, there didn't seem to be any other path to take. Marriage was inevitable: I might as well dive in now.

After ten minutes or so, I decided to change the topic. *How hard could it be to have a real conversation?* I told myself. *After all, we are just two girls talking.*

"I'm just curious," I said, "what is your favorite color?" I looked at her as if to say, *Hey, listen, we don't have much time to talk. We might as well talk about more personal things.*

"Well, I think pink is beautiful," Fraidy said with a smile. "On clothes, it isn't modest outside of the home, but I think it looks wonderful on bed linens, for example."

I smiled, too. I wanted to say that pink was my favorite as well, but I knew that it would seem weird to her, so I didn't. Instead, we moved on to talk about our favorite foods.

Before long, we were both at ease. With the ice broken, I felt relieved, and unexpectedly comfortable, and so did she. The meeting was going better than I'd expected, better even than what our parents had prepared us to expect.

We were joking about some funny relatives we had in common when Fraidy, laughing, said, "Is this what we are supposed to talk about?"

"How would I know?" I responded with a shy smile, almost a wink.

After another twenty minutes or so, Mommy came to the open dining room door to check on us.

"So, how is it going?"

"Great, I think!" we answered in unison.

We smiled as our eyes met directly for the first time.

"So, a few more minutes?" Mommy asked.

"Yes, sure!" we replied.

We talked a little longer, laughing from time to time.

As we finished talking, my eyes caught Fraidy's gaze, and a final thought ran across my mind.

I should be sitting on that side of the table. I should be the bride.

WITH ITS INTENSE focus on reproduction and family life, the Hasidic community strongly believes young people should marry at age eighteen. This is not simply a religious belief, though the biblical commandment to be fruitful and multiply is taken at face value. It's also a cultural belief, and one that is deeply entrenched in the Hasidic way of life. Just as many Americans expect their kids to go to college when they reach eighteen, the Hasidic community expects eighteen-year-olds to get engaged and be married.

There was a little leeway, but not much. Once a Hasidic child reaches twenty, their match prospects diminish. Everyone wonders why they got "so old" without finding a spouse. There was a joke that girls who are older than twenty already had a "gray braid."

Being unmarried is not just a disgrace; it influences your place in society in every way, from your standing in the synagogue to how seriously your opinion is taken on important matters. This means the social pressure to get married is extreme. In yeshiva, by the end of the fourth year, when most students are nineteen or twenty years old, about 80 percent of the students are married. Some students will then stay for another year or two; they are already known as the "old" students, and in yeshiva we called them "the Senate," and not in a respectable way. Once a student is married, it is assumed he will move on. Partly this is because it is difficult for an unmarried person to relate to a married person, and vice versa. Life becomes very different after marriage.

For girls, staying unmarried is especially problematic. After a girl finishes twelfth grade, there are few opportunities to continue studying. This leaves her at loose ends to fill her time. Girls can go to work, and many serve as teachers or secretaries in the community. But these jobs are limited. And it's not as though there is a "social life" available for young singles. Socializing across gender lines is strictly forbidden and thought to be unnecessary. The idea that two young people can meet and choose each other is foreign; instead, marriages are arranged by the parents, with the help of matchmakers.

The first thing matchmakers take into account when considering possible matches are the families. There is a complex but unwritten algorithm, so to speak, that determines a family's status within the community. Among the many factors it measures is how long both parents' families have been part of the Hasidic world—the longer the better. If even one grandparent was not raised Hasidic, or, even worse, not raised Orthodox, the candidate is automatically downgraded to third class. There are, of course, other factors that come into play, such as how devoted a family is, how much money they have, and how much community influence they enjoy. But as a whole, these benchmarks matter less than their standing in Hasidism itself.

From there, the families are placed into two different categories: rabbinic families and everyone else. There are families that straddle these two groups, with one parent rabbinic and one not, and their children often marry both ways. However, marriages between families that are fully rabbinic and families that are not are almost unheard of.

Rabbinic families can also be divided into two groups: rabbinic families and *rebbishe* families. Rabbinic families are the children and grandchildren of community rabbis and religious leaders, and families can gain or lose this status based on the occupations of the parents and grandparents. *Rebbishe* families are the families of Hasidic rebbes, the Hasidic Supreme Leaders, whose children will take over the leadership from their parents. It is nearly impossible to join the ranks of a *rebbishe* family if you aren't born into one. Every year, a list is published with the names of all the available boys and girls from *rebbishe* families. These lists often have as many as four hundred names on them, and these were the only marriage options that could be considered for my siblings and me.

Only then does the question of whether the couple is a good match on a personal level become a factor. Usually, there is an informal matrix that determines whether a boy is a "good boy," and whether a girl is a "good girl," with many intermediate levels and rankings. A good boy has a strong record of studying in yeshiva, plans to continue his studies after marriage, has good manners, and is devoted to Judaism. A good girl is one who dresses modestly, has flawless manners, possesses the skills to be a competent housewife, and is attractive but still modest—modesty is in fact one of the most essential qualities in a girl of marriageable age.

Some Hasidic parents do their best to make sure the couple is compatible; others care far more about the prestige attached. My parents, I am grateful to say, always wanted to match us with people we would get along well with, someone we would truly like.

"MOMMY ALREADY HAS pictures at home!" my brother Hershy told me. It was the end of fall 5770 (2009), and my family was visiting the yeshiva for Shabbos. Hershy and I were standing outside of the Rebbe's house, looking over the campus from his porch. Tati had told me a few weeks earlier that a matchmaker had suggested a match for me and that he was considering it. The girl was a daughter of Meir Horowitz, and they were direct descendants of the previous Viznitz'er Rebbes. I knew and liked the family. Now I was just waiting for Mommy and Tati to decide, and as part of their deliberations, they were offered photographs of the girl, whose name I still didn't know.

A few minutes later I saw Mommy, who was settling into a bedroom in the Rebbe's house. "Is it true that you have pictures?" I asked.

"Yes, and when there is more to know, we will let you know," she said.

I was probably about to get engaged, but there was nothing for me to do except wait and try to focus on my studying. I was excited that there was a possibility I could marry a Viznitz girl—and had told Tati and Mommy many times that that was my preference—but we all knew it would be a bit of a struggle. Our family's dress code was stricter than in the majority of Viznitz families, and that could make a girl's parents less interested in the match.

Over the next few days, every time I called home, I asked for an update. Finally, Tati said that he was ready to move ahead.

The next step was for Tati to visit the Rebbe. Tati always asked the Rebbe about the potential for a match, both for his agreement and his blessing. Usually Tati would call the Rebbe's house and either speak to the Rebbe directly or ask one of his grandkids to carry the message and call him back with a reply. This time, however, it was Hanukkah, and Tati was going to be in Monsey anyway. He would be in attendance when the Rebbe lit the Hanukkah candles in a public ceremony, as he was every year.

"I'll see the Rebbe on Monday," Tati said over the phone. "I'll ask him then."

Monday came and went. So did Tuesday.

On Wednesday morning, I called Tati.

"The Rebbe was enthusiastic," he said. "As soon as I mentioned you, he lit up, and he said that he has heard you are doing beautifully at yeshiva. Then I asked him about the Horowitz match, and he was excited to hear of it. He said he thinks it is a great match, and he gave his warm wishes."

That meant that for our side of the agreement, the engagement was approved. Now Meir Horowitz would ask the Rebbe, too, and get his blessing as well. And so Wednesday afternoon, before the Hanukkah candle lighting, Meir Horowitz went to the Rebbe to ask what he thought about the match.

"I hear the groom is doing very well in yeshiva," the Rebbe said. "The Stein family is a wonderful family. Mendel Stein teaches a class every day in our Williamsburg synagogue, and people like and admire him."

"So is the Rebbe giving his blessing for the engagement?" Meir asked.

The Rebbe was quiet for a minute.

"Meir, you are my family. And so are the Steins, they are also my family. So, I am too close to this to give an unbiased opinion. I cannot say."

Meir left the Rebbe's room confused. He knew the Rebbe was referring to a Talmudic law that says a family member is not eligible to be a witness—in other words, he was abstaining from making a pronouncement. But this was unprecedented. The Rebbe never actually *decided* about engagements—he never said yes or no to the match—because, according to the Talmud, that is God's domain. But we knew whether the Rebbe approved based on the tenor of his response. If he said "a wonderful match," or something similar, we knew he approved. If he didn't, he might say something like "Do you have any other possible matches to consider?" or "Isn't it too soon?"

To Meir, the Rebbe's response was ambiguous, and that was troubling. Meir was a true believer in the Rebbe's holy spirit, which gave the Rebbe divinely inspired wisdom and knowledge. There was no way he was going to move forward without the Rebbe's clear blessing.

He called the matchmaker and told him what happened.

The matchmaker called Mommy and Tati and relayed the news.

Everyone was confused.

The Rebbe had given Tati his enthusiastic blessing, but he had not offered the same to Meir. How could that be?

Tati decided to call his friend and cousin, Srulik Hager, the Rav. Srulik was the Rebbe's closest son and the rabbi of the Viznitz community in Monsey. He was also married to Mommy's first cousin.

"I am not sure what to do here," Tati told him after explaining the situation.

"This is interesting, and unusual," Srulik agreed. "Let me speak to him, and I will see what he says."

So Srulik went to the Rebbe.

"Mendel Stein was here two days ago asking about the match with Meir Horowitz, and you offered your warm wishes for the couple. But then, when Meir came, you gave him an ambiguous answer. No one is sure what to do, and there is a possibility that the match is off now."

"Oh no, oh no!" the Rebbe responded. "That is not what I meant. I do think it is a perfect match. Please relay to both sides that I said they can make the engagement with a happy heart!"

Srulik called Tati and Meir, and he relayed the Rebbe's response. The match could move ahead.

THAT THURSDAY EVENING, the entire yeshiva was scheduled to travel to Monsey to attend the Rebbe's Hanukkah candle lighting, and then we were to stay in Monsey until after Shabbos, as was the custom every year. We arrived in Monsey at around 4:00 p.m., just in time to join the Rebbe for the afternoon prayers before sunset. As usual, the students stood around the Rebbe's chair during prayers at the front of the synagogue, which was filled with a thousand Hasidim.

After the prayers, the Rebbe turned to his secretary and asked for me. I approached the Rebbe, and the Rebbe took my hand.

"Follow me into my room," the Rebbe said.

The entire synagogue watched me leave with the Rebbe, and we went to his private office. Once we were settled in the room, the Rebbe waited for his secretary to leave, and told him to close the door behind him. Then he told me what he had said to Srulik.

"I was asked about the match with Horowitz," the Rebbe said, "and I might have given conflicting answers. Please tell your father and the matchmaker that I said this is a beautiful match, and that the engagement can move ahead with happy and light hearts!"

I thanked the Rebbe and walked out of his room feeling a complicated mix of feelings. I was excited and nervous, and all I wanted to do was call home. Outside, a group of yeshiva friends were waiting for me.

"What did the Rebbe want?" they asked. "What did he say?"

I wasn't ready to talk about it and tried to deflect the inquisition.

"It was something private," I said, hoping that would put them off. Instead it annoyed them, and they grumbled at me.

THE REBBE HAD offered his good wishes, but it was still not yet time for me to meet the girl. Before a meeting could be arranged, a phone call was placed to an organization that would confirm our genetic compatibility. This was a way to lower the risk of genetic diseases, which are rampant among Ashkenazi Jews because of our common ancestry. Every sixteen-year-old in the community takes a genetic test, and as a final step before an engagement is finalized, a call is placed to make sure the boy and the girl are not both carrying one of the same genetic mutations. If they are, the match is off.

Mommy called on Monday, and we hoped to hear within a few days; we were cautioned, though, that it could take as long as a week to hear the results.

The next Monday morning, I called home first thing.

"Any updates?" I asked.

"Not yet," Mommy said.

I couldn't bring myself to think about anything else all morning. I was excited and filled with anticipation. I was also grappling with unbidden feelings that I should be the bride, not the groom. It seemed like the longer I waited, the stronger those feelings grew inside of me.

I called Tati. "Any updates?"

"Nothing has changed since you spoke to Mommy two hours ago," he teased.

"Okay, fine," I said. "I am just so anxious, waiting here!"

"You know what?" Tati said, attempting to ease my mind. "Go tell Reb Yossel that you are expecting an important phone call, and that in order to make sure I can reach you, I will call you in his office."

I went to Reb Yossel and explained the situation, as my father had told me to. While I was there, I asked him if he could give me some advice about how to act when—if!—I finally met the girl.

Reb Yossel gave me a few basic pointers, like "Don't look into her eyes," and "Address her in third person, as opposed to saying *you*." He also added, "Make sure to say good night after the engagement party."

The talk with Reb Yossel helped me relax. I walked to the study hall, took my textbook to an empty spot, and dove into my studies.

Barely twenty minutes later, Reb Yossel appeared.

"Your father is on the phone for you in my office," he said.

My stomach dropped. I could feel the knots inside of it.

"The results came back," Tati said. "Come home, it is time to get engaged!"

I WAS AN eighteen-year-old girl, living as a boy, who had just been told she was about to get engaged to a girl.

I left campus, taking a bus to the Viznitz community's village of Kaser in Monsey and another bus from there to Williamsburg. The whole way, my anxiety flipped between worrying if she would like me to questioning what I was doing, pretending to be a groom when I was a girl.

When I finally reached home, Mommy told me that the *ba-show* was being arranged, and that it would take place in Borough Park, at the home of Fraidy's sister, whose name was Malky. And so it was that around 5 p.m., on a chilly evening in

Brooklyn, Tati called a car and Mommy, Tati, and I headed to Borough Park.

Until then, the matchmaker had been the go-between for the two families at every step. According to custom, the families don't speak to each other directly until after the engagement, and arranging this meeting between the potential bride and groom was included in that practice. Which is why the matchmaker called us while we were on our way to Borough Park to say that Meir and his wife, Yiddis, were stuck in traffic and wouldn't be ready to meet us when we arrived. So instead, we headed to Zeide Stein's house, just a few blocks from Malky's apartment, to wait.

When we arrived, Zeide and Bobbe were clearly aware that a match was about to happen.

"This is going to be the third Fraidy Stein in the family!" Bobbe said, referring to Mema Fraidy, who was Tati's youngest brother's wife, and another Fraidy who was married to a cousin.

This was the first time I had heard the name of the girl I was about to meet. Fraidy is a nickname for Freida, a Yiddish name meaning "happiness." I liked that.

Soon we were alerted that the Horowitzes were ready for us, and we walked over to Malky's apartment. The *bashow* was about to begin.

Malky's apartment was small and warm, and as I walked in, I passed a small kitchen. On the countertop was a bottle of vodka and a cake, waiting to be shared once the engagement was final. I was about to meet my future wife for the first time, and celebrations had already been planned.

We all sat down around the dining room table, in three chairs on each side. I sat between Mommy and Tati, while Fraidy sat directly across from me between her parents.

All four parents knew one another quite well, and they chattered on about family and friends they had in common. Tati and Meir shared a brother-in-law, and Mommy's oldest brother, Duvid, was married to Yiddis's older sister Shifra. Finally, after about ten minutes, the parents left the room so we could talk on our own.

Forty-five minutes later, Mommy reappeared in the doorway and asked us if we were ready to move on.

We looked at each other, and I said, "We could keep talking, but then we would be here all night. So, yes, I guess we are ready."

I looked at Fraidy, her smile bright and wide.

She is cute, I thought.

Then Fraidy went to talk to her parents in the bedroom, and I went to talk with Tati and Mommy in the kitchen.

"So, what do you think?" Mommy asked.

"She seems amazing," I said.

Tati called the matchmaker. "We are ready to agree to the match, and to drink a *l'chaim*!"

A minute later the matchmaker called back. "The other side is ready as well!"

We all went into the dining room for a toast.

A *l'chaim* is the way a Hasidic engagement happens. Both families drink vodka or another kind of liquor and shake hands, and just like that, there is a bride and a groom. Customarily, there is also a small party for the families—the *vort*—so my siblings were called over, and Fraidy's siblings joined us, too.

The party was light and joyful, full of mazel tovs and wishes for a good life, and my heart warmed to the moment. That is, until a particular guest arrived, one I should have expected but hadn't looked forward to seeing again.

It was Kalmen Halberstam, my former principal, the one who had expelled me from Tzhelim.

I am sure that I started to blush.

It was no surprise that he was there. After all, he was about to become my uncle. Kalmen's wife was my future father-in-law's sister. I already knew that, but in the moment it now dawned on me that the person who was once a favorite teacher, but then became my archenemy and expelled me from school, would soon be my uncle.

After our showdown in 2008, I had hoped I would never run into Kalmen again. We had seen each other a few times, usually when I visited Mema Chaya at the camp during the summers. Our run-ins were civil, even though the tension was still in the air.

I was sitting with Tati when he approached us.

I sighed. *What now?* I thought. *Is it just going to be awkward for the rest of our lives? Is he going to tell my new in-laws about the trouble I caused?*

Instead, he greeted us with a smile.

"Mazel tov! And welcome to the family!" he exclaimed, in a tone that I think was genuine.

He turned to Tati.

"The Talmud says that every fight that is for the sake of heaven will, in the end, bring peace. There is a Hasidic teaching that says even more—'A fight that is pure, and well meaning, doesn't just end up in peace, but it ends in a loving family connection!'"

I don't know if he believed this or if he was just trying to defuse the situation and prevent future conflict. But the air was cleared, and from then on, we were friends again, just as I was with Fraidy's other uncles.

It was the closing of a circle.

After about an hour, the celebration was over.

Before we left, I went to the kitchen where the women had gathered and said to Fraidy, "Mazel tov, and good night! We will see each other on happy occasions!"

"All the same to you, and good night!" she responded.

Just like that, we were engaged. We did not speak to each other again until the wedding, a year later.

18

GRAPHIC STUDIES

"**Y**OU LAY DOWN next to her and you give her a kiss. Also, you tell her that you love her," said Srulik, the Rebbe's son. It was his job to brief me on the matter of sex so that I would be ready for my wedding night.

His face then took on a grave expression. He looked at me intently.

"Then, you wait until you are *ready*. If you feel like it is taking you too long to get *ready*, ask her if she can help you out *down below*. Then, ask her if she is ready."

Srulik looked at me, trying to gauge my reaction. Was I following what he was saying? I indicated that he should go on with his lesson.

"If she says she is ready, get on top of her. Don't worry, women like having a man lying on top of them."

At that point Srulik paused, looking even more nervous than I was. For a man who had given more than a thousand of these talks, it seemed crazy to me that he wasn't more relaxed about it. Was he this sweaty every single time?

Srulik put his hand down on the table and spread his index and middle fingers. Then he picked up a pen that was on the table and pointed it at the space in between the fingers, which I was meant to understand were a woman's legs.

"So, there are two holes here, on the bottom of a woman's body, in between her legs. Just raise yourself a bit and have her guide your *organ* into her *place*."

Now he had my attention. I knew a few of the technical details of having sex, but until that moment, I had no idea where to find the vagina. Somehow I thought it was where the belly button is. Between the legs? Really?

"Then, once you are in, just push yourself in all the way. Stay there until you are finished, and once you are finished, make sure that you leave every drop of your seed inside her. Then, get off from on top of her and lay down next to her for at least fifteen minutes. Make sure to talk with her during that time!"

I considered asking him what we should talk about, and then thought better of it.

Again, I gestured for him to continue.

"After you have spent some time lying next to her, stand up and wipe yourself off," Srulik said. "Make sure there is no blood, and if there is, have her check herself with the special cloth. Always have cloths ready. After there is blood, she is considered a *niddah*."

Niddah is a biblical word that literally means something like "exiled," but it is used by the rabbis to talk about a woman who is "impure." When a woman bleeds from the vagina, regardless of the time of month, she is considered impure to her husband, and she is exiled from him. Any form of touching each other, even to pass a glass of water, is forbidden for seven days following the sign of blood.

"Is this all clear to you?" Srulik asked.

"Yes, it is," I said, though I was still a little confused about the exact details. I couldn't quite visualize it.

"One more thing," Srulik continued. "I have a strict message from my father, the Rebbe: that if you ever come home late at night, like from a wedding, and you feel that if you don't do it you might spill your seed, you are obligated to do it! Of course, all the rules still apply."

Well, that's nice, I thought to myself. I knew about the rules of having sex twice a week, but I somehow thought that twice was the limit.

"Finally," he said, "make sure not to overdo it. I know several people who got divorced during the first year because the husband kept asking for it every night. At some point, she might just get grossed out."

THE DAY AFTER Fraidy and I got engaged, I went back to yeshiva. Back at school, I dove deeper into Kabbalah, with an ebullience I'd never felt before. For the first time in my life, I finally had some justification for my gender confusion. My soul was feminine—nothing seemed truer.

Kabbalah helped me sort out so many of my questions. I could finally learn more about how souls work from a mystical point of view, and I held tight to the Kabbalistic idea that the gender of a soul and the gender of a body don't always align. I also found all kinds of new ideas about femininity. Many Kabbalistic prayers refer to God and to the Divine in feminine language, and I felt at home with that. If I couldn't express my physical femininity, relating to the divine feminine was the next best thing.

As part of my exploration of Kabbalistic beliefs, I began learning about the importance of "the Midnight Ritual," a well-known but not widely observed Kabbalistic practice based on the Talmud. The Talmud says that since the destruction of the Temple in 70 CE, God—and, more importantly, the feminine aspect of God—has stood up every night, exactly at midnight, and cried over its destruction and over the Jews who were spread around the world. As a result of that teaching, the Kabbalists believe that every living person is also obligated to cry at midnight. We are supposed to cry not only for the destruction of the Temple, but also for the sake of the desecration of the Divine's name. Kabbalah also teaches that during that time, we have the best chance for our prayers to be answered.

I decided to do it.

Waking up at midnight every night seemed a little severe, even for me, but once a week seemed reasonable. First, though, there were a few hurdles to overcome. There were rules I'd have to break, but that only made my plan more attractive to me. I loved challenges, especially when it meant subverting authority.

The biggest obstacle was the curfew. At 10:15 p.m., we were all supposed to be in our rooms. If a student was seen at 3:30 a.m. walking the hallways, it was assumed that he had woken up early to study—but being seen in the hallways at 11:30 or midnight usually meant the student had broken curfew. So I would have to sneak out of my room.

Another hurdle was getting into the mikvah. According to the Kabbalists, it was necessary to immerse oneself in the ritual bath before consorting with the Divine. But the mikvah didn't open on Fridays until 3:30 a.m., so I'd have to break in.

The first week I couldn't find a way in; it was locked tight. The next week, however, I got help from an unlikely source—my friend Srully Adler.

Srully was a year younger than me, and, like me, he was kind of a "kosher rebel." Srully somehow managed to avoid making curfew almost nightly and get away with it. He was also one of the most intelligent students on campus, and one of the most open-minded and well-educated teenagers I had ever met. I became close with Srully in the beginning of the second year, when we teamed up to publish the monthly yeshiva magazine, of which we later became coeditors. I hadn't planned to enlist his help, but on the second week, as I snuck down the hallway toward the mikvah, I ran into him.

"Are you looking for a way into the mikvah?" Srully asked.

"Yes—but you aren't going to tell on me, are you?" I said.

"Of course not. I sneak in all the time," he said.

I sighed in relief.

"But you're not going to find an open door," he continued. "The only way in is through the roof."

The roof! That sounded fun. Talk about breaking the rules.

Srully pointed to a spot in the hallway, right above the phone booths, that provided access to the tiled roof.

"Follow me, and be careful," he said, showing me the way. "Only walk on the beams, not on the pipes or the tiles."

I followed close behind. It was quick, easy, and exhilarating.

From that week on, I woke up every Friday just before midnight, immersed myself in the mikvah, and recited the prayers of the Midnight Ritual. After that, I would head to study hall and study though the night until 8 a.m., when it was time for morning prayers.

IN ADDITION TO taking on the Midnight Ritual, I also ramped up my competitive streak. A few times a year, the yeshiva held study competitions to see who could log the most hours learning, and students would study for hours and hours without stopping for anything. We kept track of our hours and submitted them to the faculty, and then the results were delivered to the Rebbe. I racked up enough hours to top the lists.

Also once a year, there was a two-week-long study competition for Viznitz teenagers around the world, and the winner, in addition to being on top of the list taken to the Rebbe, would be known to the entire community. It was my last year of yeshiva, and I decided to win. I launched a nonstop study campaign, a marathon of learning that had me, at some points, in front of my books for twenty-two hours a day. Once, I went a full twenty-seven hours, waking up at 3:30 a.m. one Thursday morning and studying practically nonstop until 8:00 a.m. on Friday morning. I only put my books down for prayers, for five-minute food breaks, and for fast trips to the bathroom.

Then, every summer, the Rebbe would come up and spend three weeks at yeshiva, and in the days leading up to his visit, the yeshiva held a study competition as a way to prepare ourselves for being in the presence of the holy Rebbe. It was my last semester in yeshiva, and I wanted to go out with a bang. So I once again was determined to log the most hours.

For days, I studied almost without stopping. One day, I took a quick break for breakfast and a visit to the bathroom, sat down on the toilet, and fell asleep.

A few minutes later, I woke up and realized where I was. Chuckling, I stood up to stretch, and that's when I became dizzy.

Suddenly I felt a smack on the back of my head, and the next thing I knew I was lying on the floor, my head under the sink, bleeding.

I guess I fell down, I thought.

I returned to my room, where my roommate Duvid was sitting on his bed.

"Duvid, can you hand me a towel? I have a red towel on my bed, get me that one," I said.

Duvid gave me the towel and watched as I pressed it against the wound.

"What happened?" he asked, now concerned.

"Nothing, really, I just fell down and knocked my head on the sink pipe," I explained.

"Hold on. You *fell down*?" Duvid asked, suddenly alarmed. I didn't know why he was so worked up, but I learned later that he'd heard me fall—a full two minutes before I emerged from the bathroom. I'd been out cold.

He called emergency medical services, and not long after that I was in the emergency room.

I was fine, but the doctor was shocked to discover how little I'd been eating and sleeping. He lectured Mommy, who translated his English into Yiddish for me.

"Tell your child that not eating or sleeping isn't okay," he admonished. "An eighteen-year-old can't live like that!"

Mommy smiled and told the doctor, "Nah, don't worry. He's getting married in a few months, he'll be okay." Then she smoothed my brow. "Right, *Shefele*?"

Shefele. Little lamb. I still loved it when Mommy called me that. Whenever I was sick, I would call her, even if I'd just had a bad day, because I knew that as soon as she heard my voice, she would be overcome with love for me and call me her *shefele*. It was the sweetest sound I have ever heard—and maybe I was delusional, but I was convinced that every time Mommy called me *shefele*, I would start to feel better.

TOWARD THE END of the summer semester, I was back in hot water. I was caught going boating off campus in the Anawana Lake, about thirty minutes away from the yeshiva. It was toward the end of the semester, when the faculty's supervision was a little more relaxed. Some friends and I felt like taking a break, and boating sounded fun. It also broke multiple rules.

"I am not going to expel you for this," Reb Yossel said when he learned about it later. "But I strongly suggest that you don't come back next semester. You are getting married anyway, so just continue your studies at a *kollel*, where there are fewer rules. That way, there will be fewer rules for you to break!"

I didn't mind. Yeshiva was getting depressing. Chesky had gotten married in the middle of the semester, and I was taking long walks at night on the New Road by myself, sometimes crying like a baby. What can I say? I was a girl in love. I couldn't just get over my feelings for him. I missed him.

I went home, and for the next semester, fall 2010, I enrolled in the local Viznitz kollel and tried to be happy about the next chapter of my life.

Kollel is, essentially, a seminary for married students. Almost every city that has a sizable Orthodox population has at least one kollel, and most Hasidic sects have their own kollels in every city where they have satellite communities. The study structure in a kollel is very similar to that in yeshiva, though most students study law instead of Talmud. In addition, kollel has shorter study sessions, and only two a day, and they are geared toward students who have a family life while studying. A kollel pays its students. When kollels started to become common in the United States after World War II, most students got paid about $50 a week, which was the average rent for a nice city apartment at the time. However, since then, the average pay hasn't kept pace with inflation. Students earn about $400 a month, which is pocket change in New York.

Over the years, more and more students leave kollel to get jobs to support their rapidly growing families. On average, by the time a student cohort has reached twenty-five years old, only 10 percent of them are still studying in kollel. Those who do stay are usually the ones who want to become rabbis, rabbinical judges, or authors of religious books—or they have rich parents or in-laws who can support them financially.

I started at the Viznitz kollel in Williamsburg in October 2010, or Cheshvan 5771. I had finished my studies of the laws on food, ritual slaughter, and the Jewish kitchen, so I dove right into finishing my study of the laws of Shabbos. My partner was Zevi, one of my few close friends from yeshiva, and he'd recently married a girl from Williamsburg.

Almost everyone, except me, was married, and married life was part of the day-to-day chatter, and especially talk about sex. Talking about sex is taboo in the Hasidic world, particularly among the unmarried, but in kollel it was treated lightly. There were still some limits—describing the act too graphically, or offering too many details, could raise eyebrows. But for most students, this was the first time in their lives that they could talk with friends openly, and since sex itself was a very new experience, there was a lot of conversation.

And a lot of listening, for me.

AS THE WEDDING approached, I could not stop thinking that I should be the bride. I liked Fraidy, but I couldn't help feeling that she deserved to marry a real man, and so did I. When my sisters were discussing their own wedding dresses, I couldn't help feeling envious. Why couldn't I wear a gown?

Another part of me thought that after I was married—and living with, sleeping with, and spending time with a "real" girl— maybe all my feelings would magically go away. I hoped for that outcome with a renewed intensity. I guess it was my own version of "praying the gay away," although it was more like "praying the girl away."

Meanwhile, the wedding plans progressed, and two months before the big day, Tati arranged for Rabbi Yisroel Rosenberg to be my Groom Teacher. This was in addition to Srulik's final briefing described above.

Due to the nonexistence of any sex-ed before marriage, everything about sexual relationships in the Hasidic community is taught to grooms and brides in the months leading up to the wedding. While for brides there is usually a Bride Teacher, a woman who is a real specialist on sexual life, for grooms it is usually a rabbi who is a "specialist" in the Jewish laws surrounding sexual relations and other practical matters. Most of the two months leading up to the wedding is focused on the Jewish laws pertaining to married life, such as the details of what acts are not allowed while the wife is in her menstrual cycle, how to count seven clean days, how to use the ritual bath to purify oneself before returning to the marriage bed, and some advice on how to have a successful marriage. I studied these topics at Yisroel's house. The laws and calculations, especially those around when a wife was statistically likely to get her period, were complex.

Yisroel was one of the leading rabbis in the Viznitz community in Williamsburg and a close friend of Tati's. I was happy with the choice; as far as Hasidic rabbis go, Yisroel was down-to-earth and relatively open-minded.

"I had my first lesson with Yisroel Rosenberg last night," I told Zevi, my study partner, one morning. "But so far, I haven't learned anything new. I already knew everything he told me."

"Really?" Zevi asked, surprised. "There must be plenty you still don't know."

"I'm telling you, I already know everything," I argued. "I know that almost every woman will see blood the first night because the husband's penis breaks the hymen." While this statement might be scientifically dubious, it's what Hasidic people are inclined to believe.

Zevi looked shocked. "Wow, you really read stuff that you are not supposed to. Those are the kinds of things you aren't supposed to know about until a few days before the wedding."

"I also know that many men aren't able to accomplish it on the first night," I added.

"Well, yeah, like only if you are really big and she is really small," Zevi said.

I nodded.

For some reason that conversation further convinced me that a vagina is somewhere on the stomach around the belly button.

Over the next two months, we continued to talk about everything relating to sex. Our conversation often got graphic, and Zevi and I shared our sexual fantasies with each other. We came up with different sexual positions that we thought might be fun for us or our sexual partners, and talked about possible ways to make sure that our wives would enjoy sex just as much as we did.

"There has to be love attached," Zevi told me one morning. "If there isn't, it is just a physical joy. Even very good sex is just like eating a very good ice cream. After a while, you will both get bored."

That escalated into a conversation about fidelity in marriage, and then about the religious laws of extramarital sex.

"Having sex outside of marriage is one of the harshest sins from God's perspective!" I said.

"Maybe for a woman," Zevi responded, "but for a man, Jewish law actually does allow men to have more than one wife and allows concubines."

I couldn't argue with that. The laws are sexist to their core, but they are the Talmudic laws. Nevertheless, most Hasidic Jews acknowledge that although the letter of the law permits polygamy—and even sex with unmarried women, as long as they have immersed themselves in the mikvah—from a cultural perspective it is a terrible thing to do.

I had no plans to have extramarital sex, but I loved hearing Zevi make his point. Only someone who is open-minded, who questions the Hasidic communal values, would say something like that.

A NIGHT OR two before the wedding, and no sooner, grooms are taught about the simple logistics of how to have sex. There are many stories of students freaking out, fainting, or refusing to believe that observant Jews could do something so lewd.

After we got married, Fraidy told me that one of her aunts had been told only the bare minimum about purity and almost nothing about sex before her wedding. Her Bride Teacher only told her, "When you get home from the wedding, it will be time to do the mitzvah. Your husband will guide you through it, and you just do as he says."

When Fraidy's aunt got home, her husband started telling her about what they were about to do: that they would remove all of their clothes, get into bed together, and do "the act."

Her aunt listened to it all, and then she ran out of the house and straight to her brother's house, as her father was deceased.

"My husband is evil," she screamed. "He wants me to do the most immodest acts possible!"

"No, no," her brother had to tell her. "Now that you are married, this is what you have to do!"

Understandably, growing up in one of the most gender-segregated communities in the world, in which we are told from a young age that just talking to the "opposite" sex is forbidden, it is sometimes hard to wrap the head around the idea that sex isn't just okay, but required.

For me, it was quite obvious from a young age that married people did something with their bodies, even if I didn't know exactly what. This is probably true for many other Hasidic people. I mean, after all, babies have to be made somehow.

There was a story that I heard when I was engaged, though I could never confirm it, that once upon a time, when a groom was learning about the basics of sex, with Srulik as his teacher, he seemed astonished and could not believe that sex was a real thing Hasidic people did.

Srulik just couldn't believe that the groom was so surprised. "What did you think, that you put on a ring and you have babies? Of course, you have to do something physical!"

To many unsuspecting grooms, Srulik would say, "The Rebbe did it, I did it, your parents did it. Even the Baal Shem Tov did it. Even Moses the prophet did it!"

In the Viznitz community, it was Srulik who gave that final talk to grooms a day or two before the wedding, usually around the same time that the bride went to the mikvah for the first time. While anyone could hypothetically teach a groom about sex, the Rebbe felt that having someone who was older, and a rabbi, was more fitting.

I met with Srulik on a Sunday morning, the day before the wedding, to have my final lesson, the one that would tell me exactly what to do. We sat in the Viznitz Williamsburg synagogue at a table in the northeast corner of the main sanctuary.

"How much about it do you know already?" Srulik started.

I decided to be honest.

"I know that I have to go inside her," I said. "I am just not sure where that hole is."

Srulik looked at me, somewhat surprised, and started with his lesson.

"When you get home, get ready for bed. Prepare water next to your bed, and make sure that it is pitch dark in the room. If there is any light shining in from the outside, cover the window with a garbage bag. And, of course, only do the mitzvah at night, ideally after sunset."

Observing my facial expressions to make sure I was following, he continued.

"Take off all your clothes, and only keep on your *tzitzit*." Tzitzit is a fringed ritual garment that is worn by men at all times under their clothing.

"Ask her to remove all of her clothes as well. It is important that during the mitzvah, your bodies touch without anything in between. It is a Kabbalistic requirement."

From there, he explained the mechanics of entry, using his fingers and the pencil.

And then the lesson was complete.

When I got home, Tati pulled me aside.

"So, how do you feel? Do you think you are ready and that you understand all the details? If not, tell me, and I will ask Yisroel Rosenberg to go over it with you."

Well, a refresher couldn't hurt.

"I am almost clear, but maybe I should talk with him anyway," I told Tati.

"Okay, sure, I'll call him," Tati said.

That night I met with Yisroel in his office at the synagogue, and he said very much the same thing as Srulik, with one minor addition.

"There are two holes," Yisroel said. "Go in the upper one and push as far as you can. Don't worry, you are not puncturing the liver or intestines."

I nodded and thanked him.

I was as ready as I would ever be.

19

A WEDDING IN A BLIZZARD

"ARE YOU FEELING okay now?" I asked my new wife.

"Yes, I just had a reaction to some Benadryl I'd taken," Fraidy said.

"I'm glad, I was worried when you left the celebration," I said.

"I'm much better," she said. "I'm really happy to be on the way home, though—on the way to *our* home," she added with the sweetest of smiles.

We were on our way from our wedding in Williamsburg to our new apartment in Monsey, and we had an hour-long drive ahead of us. Our driver was one of Tati's devoted students, Yoely Weiss, who had a van with four-wheel drive. He had generously offered to take us because it was the only way to ensure we could get there safely in the blizzard that had erupted the day before.

"You know," Fraidy said, "when we walked into the hall for the dancing, I had no idea that you would hold my hand in public. My family doesn't do that."

"Really?" I asked, surprised. "Everyone in my family does—the only time a couple ever holds hands in public is between the ceremony and the celebrations."

"Yes, my family holds hands on the way out of the ceremony, just not on the way into the dancing," Fraidy explained.

"Did you mind at all that we did? I had no idea that your family doesn't."

"No, not at all!" Fraidy laughed. "I liked it! It felt nice."

A thought crept into my head. *My new wife cares about feelings, maybe even more than she cares about every small detail of strict family customs. This is a good sign that we will get along, that we will like each other.*

It was a happy thought.

We talked all the way home. I was sure that for two people who had only met once, a year ago, there were bound to be a few awkward silences, but there weren't. We chatted, we joked, we smiled, and we held hands, and I felt much closer to her than I expected I would.

Finally, we arrived at our new apartment.

We stepped out of the car, and Yoely carried our bags inside. I helped Fraidy hold up her gown, and together we made our way into our new home. As we went, I had a feeling I could not describe. My stomach was full of butterflies, but I felt a happiness, a kind of peace and safety, I had never experienced before.

It was a feeling of love. I loved my wife.

A HASIDIC WEDDING is not just a one-night affair. Every Hasidic wedding begins the weekend before—or, more precisely, the Shabbos before. Celebrating the Groom's Shabbos and the Bride's Shabbos dates back to Talmudic times, but it has taken on a whole new meaning in the Hasidic world. These customs are partly based on a Kabbalistic teaching from the Zohar, a thirteenth-century collection of writings that serves as the basis of Jewish mysticism, which says that "all the blessings from above and below for the week to come hang on the seventh day." On that pre-wedding Shabbos, while the groom and the bride are still living in their parents' houses, both sides rejoice in different ways, though the bigger celebrations are on the groom's side.

On that Shabbos, the groom wears the new clothes that married men wear. It is the first time he wears the *shtreimel*, the fur hat of a married man, for instance.

In my family, the groom at this point also starts wearing many of the uniquely royal rabbinic garments exclusive to rabbinic families, such as the *strokes*, the silk coat adorned with velvet stripes, the checkered pants, and a white vest.

In the week before the Groom's Shabbos, as part of the "changing of the hats," there is a tradition where his family and close friends jokingly hit his old "unmarried" hat off his head and wish him well. It is all in good fun, and it's an uplifting way to mark the end of the single years.

For me, as that day approached, my feelings about my gender started encroaching on my joy. In the buildup to the wedding, I tried my best to focus on the exciting parts of getting married—and on hoping that my marriage would somehow negate the feeling of being a girl. But while I rejoiced along with my family in many ways, I found that any aspects of our wedding that were uniquely "manly"—anything that signified that I was the groom instead of the bride—hit me hard.

"Are you ready for this week's Shabbos?" my brother Hershy asked me in the middle of the week. "Have you decided which hat you are going to wear to synagogue? I mean, you have to make sure it's an old one, because if everyone is going to hit you, it will be ruined forever."

This was supposed to be fun, a welcome distraction before all the seriousness of the wedding. Not for me.

All I could think was that the *bride* doesn't have an entertaining hat ritual. Heck, she doesn't even wear a hat.

"I think I want to go away this Shabbos," I told Tati on Wednesday. "After the busyness of all the wedding preparations, I need some time away, a quiet weekend."

"Okay," Tati said. "Why don't you go to Zeide Stein's house?"

Zeide lived directly upstairs from his synagogue, and spending Shabbos there meant avoiding friends and brothers who might want to hit my hat, along with all the other well-wishers who would want to talk about this being my last Shabbos before marriage.

It was an escape from the reality that I was a groom and not a bride.

THE SHABBOS BEFORE the wedding is supposed to be one of the happiest and most peaceful times in the life of every Hasidic groom, and that is exactly what shook me to the core.

All the groom's siblings, uncles, and cousins, along with many friends and community members, gather on Saturday morning. The groom is called to the Torah with a special song marking the occasion of the wedding. After reading a few verses from the Torah, the men sing another traditional wedding song, and the women, standing behind a wall or in a gallery, toss down small bags filled with snacks and candies. This tradition is more than a thousand years old, and it symbolizes many things, among them the sharing of joy and wishes for a sweet life.

While I imagine that many Hasidic grooms might feel anxious during that time—an understandable emotion before anyone begins a new life—I felt something else entirely. Instead of feeling nervous about the upcoming ceremony and marital life, and reveling in the festivities, all I could think about were the different roles for men and women, and how I was on the wrong side. I couldn't enjoy any of it.

Just as I had many times in the past, when the dissonance between who I was and what was happening to me grew too stark, I soon blacked the memories out of my consciousness. As a result, I have only a few clear recollections of the weekend.

I remember having the *shtreimel* placed on my head for the first time by the Rebbe, who was in Williamsburg for the Shabbos before my wedding.

I remember that he held my hand as we walked from his room into the main sanctuary of the synagogue.

I remember that after the service, we headed to a small nearby venue, where my family and Fraidy's brothers came to celebrate with me. I sat at the head table, glancing over to the women's section, where my sisters wore beautiful knee-length dresses. I envied them.

I remember losing my cool with Zeide Stein while we waited for the meal to begin. I was hungry and overwhelmed, and I lashed out about why everything was taking so long. "This is supposed to be about me, but it feels like it is about everyone else!" I complained.

That was my way of saying, *If this were about me, we would be having a Shabbos for a bride.*

And I remember eavesdropping on my sisters as they chatted about the Shabbos on the bride's side. They talked about how the groom's family, as well as many friends, send the bride flowers, and on Friday night before dinner, the bride's friends come over to sing and celebrate together, a Hasidic version of a bachelorette party.

It sounded lovely.

Admittedly, my weekend had nice moments, too. The whole family—my twelve siblings, five in-laws, and about ten nieces and nephews—came together. When I look back on my young life, and think about our times together as a cozy family, that weekend is one of my favorite memories, despite all the things that troubled me at the same time.

OUR WEDDING WAS held on Monday, December 27, 2010—or, as we knew it, the 20th day of the Hebrew month of Tevet 5771.

In my family, it is a fairly common practice for the women to have professional pictures taken at a wedding. On the men's side, though, that was rarely done. Having professional photos taken was seen as too feminine; they were also thought to distract the groom from the important moments of the wedding itself that he should be focusing on.

In the Viznitz community, this was especially true. The Rebbe hated pictures. He saw photography as a modern concept, one that had gotten out of control, and he had a strict prohibition against anyone photographing him, ever. In a world where every phone has a camera, and a camera can be the size of a pen, of course it is almost impossible to avoid having one's picture taken in public. But the Rebbe managed to maintain an impressive degree of control over this, and few pictures were ever taken of him. They do exist, but for a leader of thousands of people, the number is very small.

The Rebbe rarely prohibited pictures from being taken of other people, but he hated pictures at weddings with a special passion. As a way to encourage people not to take photographs, he had a standard offer: for every wedding where both sides agreed not to take any pictures, he would personally attend the wedding and dance with the bride and groom. For followers of the Rebbe, having him at the wedding—dancing with the newlyweds and giving his blessings in person—was a worthwhile tradeoff, and the obvious choice for most Viznitz Hasidim.

In our case, both families agreed right away not to hire a photographer, and we were all excited to know the Rebbe would be at the wedding, myself especially.

Then, on Sunday, as I was meeting with Yisroel Rosenberg in his room at the synagogue to review the lessons of my Groom Teacher, Srulik stopped by.

"My father said that he will not only come to the wedding and dance, but he will also officiate at the ceremony!"

Now I was really thrilled. At most weddings in the community that he attended, the Rebbe recited blessings, but he did not oversee the ceremony. This had only happened for his own grandchildren's weddings and a few others. And now he'd be doing so for mine! I was delighted. With all the hubbub around me, and my inner turmoil, having the Rebbe there made me feel that I was on the right path. It centered me.

As the Yiddish saying goes, "A man thinks and God laughs." I didn't believe in a God who was sitting somewhere watching over humanity and laughing. But if I had, I would have been really angry at him. Because on Sunday, the day before the wedding, New York City was hit with one of the harshest snowstorms in memory. In a matter of hours, twenty-six inches of snow covered the streets, paralyzing the city that never sleeps. Then, on top of the storm, the sanitation department went on strike, and it took more than a week before all the streets were cleared.

The Rebbe couldn't come.

When I heard the news, my heart dropped. It compounded all the feelings I already had that my marriage was wrong—that I was not ready, that I was too young, that I was marrying as the wrong gender.

Then, the day of the wedding, Fraidy got sick.

There is a Hasidic custom that the bride and groom fast on the day of the wedding. It is seen as their personal day of atonement, and not everyone takes to fasting the same way. For Fraidy, it was a grueling experience. On top of that, the night before the wedding, she used a facial cream that she had never used before and had an allergic reaction to it. In the morning, her whole face was bright red.

While I was locked in my room reciting the Book of Psalms, as is the custom for the bride and groom on the day of the wedding, I could hear Mommy on the phone.

"As long as it is just concealer, we don't mind!" she said.

Fraidy's mother wanted Fraidy to use makeup to cover the redness. In both of our families, wearing makeup on any day was considered immodest, but wearing makeup on the wedding day, the holiest day of one's life, was unthinkable. So she called Mommy to make sure she was okay with Fraidy using concealer to cover the rash. Mommy agreed—as long it was only concealer and nothing else, heaven forbid.

So Fraidy wore the makeup, and she also took Benadryl, which wasn't the best thing for an empty stomach.

We were not off to a good start.

AT FIRST, MY mystic brain wanted to attribute all our problems to a divine sign that everything about this was wrong. But on the ride home after the wedding, talking and sharing stories from the night, and from our lives, something changed inside of me. The more we spoke, the more I liked Fraidy, and the more she liked me. Something sweet was growing between us.

That night, we consummated the marriage as we were told we must, and it went well under the circumstances, considering that it was her first time being intimate with someone and my first time with the "opposite" sex. We settled into our new lives with a kind of happiness that momentarily quelled my anxieties.

In the weeks following our wedding, I dug even deeper into Jewish mysticism. Soon I was on another high from it—this time from all that I was learning about erotic mysticism. In Kabbalah, sexual relationships on Earth are believed to correspond with the intimate cosmic relationship happening between the divine God and Goddess. The Kabbalah teaches that a successful and holy intimacy between a human couple helps to create a better world in the cosmos.

In my marriage to Fraidy, I was sure I had found my place in the world, above and below. I had finally come of age, I thought. I had finally become an adult, and grown out of my feelings of being a girl.

Except I hadn't.

I still *knew* that I was a girl. I just thought that I could finally, truly, suppress it. And it worked—for a while.

But a man thinks and reality laughs.

I was a girl, and nothing could change that. Mysticism could help me bury it for a while, and it could help me subdue my religious questioning. But I was living that life on borrowed time.

All it would take was the smallest thing to burst my bubble, and my entire life would explode out of it.

Four months after our wedding, it happened. Fraidy was pregnant. We were expecting our first child.

Oh, and gender? It started punching me in the face.

20

ANOTHER CHILD

"**S**HE JUST SAW blood," my mother-in-law said, coming out of the room where Fraidy was in labor. It was 5:00 a.m., and we'd been at the hospital for two hours. "So be careful not to touch her anymore. I'll help her with anything she needs."

From that moment on—through the morning and into the day—as Fraidy's contractions grew closer together and more painful, there was little I could do to help her. After the sighting of blood, she was considered a *niddah*, and I wasn't allowed to touch her, or to see any private part of her body. Because of these restrictions, the custom is for a husband not to be in the delivery room while his wife is giving birth, since it would be close to impossible to avoid seeing things you aren't supposed to. I was close to useless.

"I guess now would be a good time for you to go to the mikvah," Fraidy told me. According to the Kabbalistic teachings and Hasidic custom, it is important for the husband to go to the mikvah and immerse himself in the ritual bath while his wife is in labor. He is to use that time to say a prayer for a speedy delivery and a healthy child.

I left the hospital and took the bus from the Good Samaritan Hospital in Suffern back to our apartment in Spring Valley.

"Fraidy just started bleeding," I told Mommy over the phone on the bus, "so I'm heading home to go to the mikvah."

"Good idea," Mommy said. "The best thing you can do now is say a wholehearted prayer and ask God for a healthy baby, a boy or a girl!"

Then she handed the phone to Tati.

"How is it going?" Tati asked.

"So far everything is going well," I said. "She has been having intense contractions, and now they are two minutes apart."

Tati had put his phone on speaker so that Mommy could hear as well.

"That's normal," Mommy interjected. "Even the early bleeding is quite common, especially for a first child."

"She's only two centimeters dilated, though," I said, "and she has been laboring for hours already. I feel really bad for Fraidy. I don't know how she can keep up with the pain. It's so unfair that she has to go through all of that pain while I'm feeling none of it."

"Ha, men would never be able to survive that kind of pain," Mommy said with a dry laugh. She always used to say that if couples could take turns giving birth, no one would ever have more than three children: the wife would have the first, then the husband would have the second, but he wouldn't be able to bear the pain. So after his wife had one more, they would never have another. Mommy was a feminist in her own way, and she really believed in the superior powers of women.

Yes, maybe men could not survive that kind of pain, I thought to myself. *But I am a girl, so I could.* I loved Fraidy, and it was hard for me to see her suffering.

"Did you call to the Rebbe's house to ask for his blessing?" Tati asked.

"Yes."

The Rebbe could always be reached when we needed him, at any hour, even on Shabbos and holidays. On those days, there were hired non-Jews who minded the phones so that if there was a life-or-death emergency, and someone had a need for the Rebbe's blessing, they could reach him. In our community, the belief in the Rebbe's divine powers was so strong that we were convinced the Rebbe's blessing could save a life. This meant that breaking the prohibition against using electricity on the holy day was allowed, even encouraged. Late at night, someone was always awake in the Rebbe's foyer to pick up the phone if someone called.

A week before Fraidy went into labor, the Rebbe took one of his extremely unusual vacations. Most Hasidic rebbes take a few vacations each year, but this was the Rebbe's first in eight years—and he agreed to take it only because his doctor had told him he needed it. The Rebbe was now eighty-nine years old, and he was weakening. So the Rebbe had gone to a vacation home on the Jersey Shore, and that's where he was when I spoke to him on the phone and asked for his blessing.

As soon as I arrived home, I grabbed my prayer shawl and headed to the mikvah. After the mikvah, I went to the synagogue to pray the morning prayers.

As soon as I was done, I took the bus back to the hospital.

About a minute into the ride, my mother-in-law called.

"Are you on your way back?" she asked.

"Yes, I just left."

"Good," she said. "We have a problem."

I felt my heart skip a beat, my stomach knotting up.

"What's going on?"

"The doctor is having a bit of trouble picking up the baby's heartbeat," she said.

I was terrified. A tear fell down my cheek.

"The doctor said that he is almost certain everything is okay," she continued. "This happens from time to time. But he thinks a Cesarean section might be a good option. We need to decide."

A Cesarean section wasn't what we wanted. We knew the recovery could be more complicated from a Cesarean. Given that this was our first child, if it was a boy it also meant missing out on a particular celebration on the baby's thirtieth day of life. The Bible requires every firstborn son who is not from a priestly family to be "redeemed" on that day, and we marked the occasion with a beautiful ceremony. But that only happened when the baby had been born in a natural birth. If the child came into the world in any way other than through the birth canal, the obligation to redeem—and to celebrate—is nulled.

"Okay," I told Fraidy's mother. "I will call the Rebbe and ask him what we should do."

Yes, it was that simple. When we didn't know what to do, there was always a solution: ask the Rebbe, who would tell us the divine will. There was a kind of certainty in knowing that every important question could be answered in this way, by deferring to the Rebbe, and to his holy spirit. It is an indescribable comfort that I sometimes still envy.

I called the number I'd been given to reach the Rebbe.

My cousin Chaim Meir, one of the Rebbe's grandchildren, picked up.

"Do you have good news yet?" he asked me. "The Rebbe has been asking since the moment you called."

"Well, the opposite, actually," I told him, and I relayed what the doctor said.

"Okay, let me ask the Rebbe what to do," Chaim Meir said.

I heard him walk to the Rebbe's room and then speak to the Rebbe: "My cousin Mendel Stein's child is on the phone again," he said. "The doctor says that there might be a need for a Cesarean section, and they want to know what to do."

I couldn't hear the Rebbe's response, but after a minute, Chaim Meir came back on the line.

"The Rebbe says that if the doctor says that this might be needed, then they should do it."

We had our answer. Then I called Fraidy's mother to tell her what the Rebbe had said.

A few minutes later, the doctor started preparing for surgery.

I arrived at the hospital just as the nurses were wheeling Fraidy's bed into the operating room.

"Make sure to say psalms," Fraidy called to me in a weak voice.

I smiled at her.

"The Rebbe said it will all be okay. I will see you and the baby soon, and I will be outside the door the whole time!"

Fraidy smiled back, with her beautiful smile.

"I'll come out and tell you as soon as there is good news," the doctor assured me. He was a Modern Orthodox Jew, and unfazed that I hadn't come with Fraidy into the delivery room. He knew the Hasidic practices.

They rolled her away, leaving me in the dimly lit corridor of the maternity ward, waiting for the doctor to come out of the room where my wife was giving birth to our child.

I was twenty years old.

My mind was swarming with all kinds of thoughts, some of which I'm sure other new parents can relate to. *Will I be a good parent? Am I ready to raise a child? Is the child going to be healthy? How do I make sure that I am giving this child the happiest life possible? Will Fraidy recover quickly and easily?*

The thoughts wouldn't stop.

Am I ready to be a parent? Is any young couple in our community ready when they have their first child?

I knew that our families would be there to help, and that was at least a bit reassuring.

I paced, nervously jumping between saying prayers and questioning whether I believed in prayer.

Half an hour later, the doctor came out of the room. He pulled off his gloves and turned to me with a genuine smile.

"Mazel tov! It's a boy!" he said. "Fraidy is doing well, and I believe she will make a speedy recovery!"

I was relieved and overcome.

"Are you sure?" I asked the doctor. "Are you sure it's a boy?"

Of all the possible things I could have said, this was not what he expected. It was probably the first time the doctor, who had surely delivered hundreds of babies, had heard such a question after delivering happy news.

Are you *sure* it's a boy?

The doctor looked at me as if I had just been released from the psychiatric ward.

My life had prepared me to ask such a question.

"Of course it is!" he replied, and with that he walked off.

A few minutes later, a nurse came out to say that Fraidy was all covered up and I could go into the room.

Inside, Fraidy was smiling like I had never seen her smile before, and she was holding a bundle in her arms.

I walked closer, my eyes tearing up.

"How are you feeling?" I asked her.

"I have felt better," she said, "but I have never been happier. You should hold him!"

She handed the baby to a female nurse, who handed him to a male nurse, who handed him to me.

Everything around me disappeared.

The nurses bustled around Fraidy, cleaning up the room. Various visitors came in and out, asking questions and sharing their blessings with us. Fraidy's sister called and shouted her well-wishes over the speakerphone, under the bright lights of the hospital room.

For me, it all faded away.

I gazed at the baby in my arms and felt a kind of love I had never felt before, and have not felt since. It was as though I were holding a part of myself.

I gave him a kiss on the forehead.

"I promise you, I promise you, for as long as I am alive, I will do everything in my power to make sure you have the best life possible," I whispered into his ear.

21

THE DONE THING

AFTER GETTING MARRIED, for the first time in my life, I found myself living with a woman I wasn't biologically related to.

I loved Fraidy's clothes, her colorful underwear and pink nightgowns, her cute black and navy shoes, and her beautiful black dresses. I loved her perfume, the smell of it, how it made me feel, and the pretty crystal bottle it came in. I envied her jewelry—the pearl necklace, the gold-and-diamond watch, and the white-gold bracelets.

I used her shampoos and deodorant, and I secretly even wore her underwear a few times.

I loved Fraidy, and I wanted to be with her. But I also wanted to be her.

Not her, exactly, but I wanted to be the woman—I wanted to be the wife.

In the first few months of our marriage, I tried to tell myself that my desire for her things was a sign of my desire for her. But as time passed, as I tried to understand what made my wife a woman and what made me a man, I knew that wasn't true.

I soon realized that almost all the gender norms that society enforces, especially in our community, which was so radically segregated by gender, were entirely subjective and invented by society. Years later, I learned the common term for that: *social construct*. At the time, though, it was simply *s'past nisht*, which translates to "not appropriate," and it referred to community norms that could not necessarily be explained with facts or logical reasoning. I saw them all the time, and they puzzled me. Why can't men cook and clean at home? Why can't women lead a household? Why do women have to follow the customs of their husbands' families? And so on.

Three months after we got married, forty days had passed since my wife's last period. At the instruction of our family rabbi, we had bought an early pregnancy test. It tested positive: we were about to become parents.

After notifying the Rebbe so he could pray for us, and after telling our parents, I had a conversation with the rabbi about the laws, norms, and customs surrounding pregnancy and childbirth. One of the rules I was taught was that our custom was not to ask the doctor what the baby's gender was before the birth, such as during an ultrasound. If the doctor wanted to share, we should say that we didn't want to know.

The reasons for that were mostly mystical, and in part it reflected a distrust of modern medicine.

At home, Fraidy was disappointed. She wanted to know so we could know what kind of clothes and baby gear to buy. "Do we order a pink or blue snowsuit?" she asked.

The weeks and months leading up to my son's birth were exciting and challenging at once. There I was, getting ready to raise a child of my own, and right away the gender of my child became the centerpiece of the experience. Family and friends speculated, guessing whether it was a boy or a girl by the way Fraidy was carrying the child. "If it's a boy . . . " "If it's a girl . . . " were phrases I heard over and over and over.

All I could think was, *What if my child is like me?*

And then, *We might all be wrong.*

FRAIDY STAYED AT the hospital for four days, and I slept there every night. While most Hasidic men I knew would spend just a few hours with their wives at the hospital during the day and then go home to sleep in their own beds, I wanted to stay. Part of it was out of love and a desire to help Fraidy with the baby. I wanted to spend more time with her and our newborn.

But part of me wanted to experience the female part of giving birth, the maternal part. I wasn't just another father. I was a father who was a mother internally. I know, I know—I didn't go through labor and delivery—but feelings don't care about that, and my maternal instincts were in high gear.

When we left the hospital, we went to stay with my in-laws so Fraidy could have her mother's support during the first few weeks of motherhood—a common custom in the Hasidic community, where girls are often still teenagers when they have their first child. In fact, at the time of our son's birth, Fraidy was indeed still a teenager. She turned twenty a few months after she delivered.

At the same time, I was planning the celebrations that accompany the birth of a boy.

We had a Friday night gathering called *Shulem Zucher*— literally, "peace of the boy." Our friends and family gathered at synagogue after the Shabbos meal, where they were served beans, chips, and kugel and sang celebratory songs. And, of course, they gave their best wishes for the newborn child and his parents.

Then there was the meal the night before the circumcision, called *Vach Nacht*, or "night of watching." On the eve of our son's eighth day—the night before the morning when he was to be circumcised, in accordance with biblical law—hundreds of people joined my family and in-laws for a light meal and to give their blessings for the next day.

At the circumcision, as I stood next to the Rebbe, naming my newborn son, it all came crashing down on me. It was at that moment, as I was naming my newborn "boy," that I felt my world collapsing.

My twenty years of struggling with my gender identity clashed with my son's first gendered milestone. My struggles with religion clashed with the most physical part of our religious way of life: a physical cut in the name of God, in observance of the second commandment in the Bible, named literally for our "bond" with the Jewish and biblical God.

It pushed me over the edge.

22

WIRELESS CONNECTIONS

M Y TIME HAD come. I decided to look for answers, and I turned to the one place I could think of that might offer them: the Internet.

I had never been online before, but I was aware of how the Internet worked. Thanks to the endless battle the Hasidic community had put up against the Internet since its inception, a rejection of its impure ways only intensifying as it became a household resource around the turn of the twenty-first century, we were taught exactly how it worked so we could stay away from it.

I knew there was a wireless connection to a network, because we were told that every digital device that had Internet capabilities must be brought into special community organizations to block all signals, or, as they called it, "make it kosher."

So I borrowed a tablet from a friend. He'd been rebellious enough not to bother putting the kosher filter on it, but I doubt he'd ever connected it to the Internet before. I took it to a local strip mall, hoping to find a Wi-Fi connection.

I found one, and in the perfect place: a single-stall bathroom at a small shopping center in Monsey, called Monsey Hub. Four bars were showing.

I spent days in that bathroom.

The first thing I ever Googled was the phrase "boy turn into girl." I wasn't expecting any results, and as I sat in the tiled vestibule with the smell of office washing supply coming from the mop stashed in the corner, I thought:

I am not going to find anything.

I am the only person in the world who would ask this question.

I still have to try.

My English was close to nonexistent, and besides the alphabet, the numbers, and words like yes and no, I couldn't read or speak the language. But I found the Hebrew Wikipedia page for the "Transgender" entry. In an interesting twist of coming full circle, as I am writing this in 2019, some of my own work and research on the topic of transgender and Judaism are quoted on that exact Wikipedia page—the page that first taught me the word *transgender*.

That page led me to an Israeli forum website called Tapuz, where I was introduced to other transgender people for the first time. I was still panicking about the possibility of transition—often I couldn't bear to think about it—but for the first time in my life I found other people like me.

Later, as my English improved, I found a website called Beginning Life Forums, where I posted about my experience and began meeting other trans people for the first time.

Thanks to a sister forum on Tapuz called Off the Derech, in Hebrew, which was dedicated to people leaving the Orthodox community, I learned about Hillel, an Israeli nonprofit that supports people who want to leave the Ultra-Orthodox community.

After a phone call to Hillel, I learned about Footsteps, an amazing New York–based nonprofit that supports people who are leaving the Hasidic community as well as other Ultra-Orthodox communities. At that point, I didn't join Footsteps. Joining a formal organization, even one that would help me leave, would have made it feel too real. I wasn't yet ready to take that step.

A few days into my Internet exploration, I found a website called Daat Emet. The name roughly translates to "True Opinion" or "True Knowledge." It was in Hebrew, and it was run by none other than Yaron Yadan, the former rabbi-turned-atheist whose work I'd read back in yeshiva.

After hours of research, days of revelations, and hundreds of back-and-forth emails with rabbis who promised me they would answer all the questions I had about Judaism, I finally felt comfortable enough to make the decision that Reb Mendelovitz threatened I would eight years before.

I was going off the *derech*.

THE SATURDAY AFTER that was the first time I used my phone on Shabbos, breaking the prohibition against using electricity on the day of rest.

The next fast day—the Fast Day of Esther—I ate a tuna bagel.

The following Yom Kippur, I had bacon.

I'd begun a two-year process in which I first rejected everything Jewish and then later found my way back, on my own terms. I found my gender identity in my own way, too.

Today I am proudly Jewish, and proudly transgender.

That May I opened my first Facebook account. I'd thought Facebook was a dating site, but had recently learned that it was a place to find like-minded people. I logged in and joined the Off the Derech Facebook group.

Then I emailed Footsteps and received a prompt reply from a remarkable young woman named Alex, a social worker who helped me schedule an intake appointment.

The next day I was on a train to Manhattan.

Footsteps' existence felt like a dream come true. This organization saved my life, literally and figuratively, just as it has saved the lives of hundreds of others who have left the Hasidic and Ultra-Orthodox communities. Nothing that I have accomplished in life over the past seven years—getting my first job, earning my high school equivalency diploma, being accepted to Columbia University—would have been possible if not for their work. Without the support of others, it is so much harder to leave the Hasidic community, and it can be close to impossible to succeed after leaving. Many of us who have built lives for ourselves after leaving Hasidism have Footsteps to thank for everything, including our very survival.

In November 2012, I created a Facebook account with a female persona. I named her Chavi, the Hebrew name and Yiddish nickname for the biblical Eve. Later that month, as I discovered transgender support forums and online groups, I started using the screen name "Eve."

I was finally ready. Ready to become Eve.

EPILOGUE

This is known according to the *Sod* [Mysticism] of reincarnation, that at times, a female will be in a male body,
because in the reasons of *gilgal* [reincarnation] the soul of a
female would come to be in a male.

—Rabbi Yechiel Michel of Zolochiv (1731–1786),

MY ANCESTOR

"Tati, there is something I need to talk to you about, something important," I said. It was November 9, 2015, and I
was calling him from my apartment on the Upper West Side
of Manhattan, where, to my parents' dismay, I was studying at
Columbia University.

Over the phone line, I heard him pause.

"What is it about?" he asked.

"It's something I can't talk about over the phone. Can we
meet to talk in person?"

"Okay, but can you tell me anything at all?" Tati asked.

"Well," I hesitated, "do you remember when I was a teenager
and you said you thought I was hiding something serious, something existential?"

"Yah, yah," Tati said, losing patience.

"You were right. And I'm ready to tell you what it is," I said. "But it is something really big, and I will need you to listen to me carefully. And I want to tell you myself, in person, before it becomes public."

Tati was quiet, but he agreed to see me. We agreed to meet a few days later, and I told him I'd text him the address where we'd meet.

"Can Mommy come, too?" I asked. "I think it's important for her to be there also."

"No," Tati said, his voice insistent. "I want to hear first what this is about, and then I'll decide what, and how, to tell her."

I wasn't surprised by this, but I was disappointed.

"Fine," I agreed. "But she'll know eventually."

TWO YEARS HAD passed since I'd left home and the Hasidic community. I still spoke with Tati and Mommy every day, though they weren't happy with me. They were angry and bewildered by the choices I'd made—to divorce Fraidy, to earn my GED and apply to college, to leave behind the ritual prayers and clothing and lifestyle of our family in favor of a more secular existence. Our calls were often fraught with tension, and I knew that Tati thought that staying in touch with me would eventually bring me back home, and back to Hasidic life. It was a hope I did as little as possible to encourage.

"Did you hear the story about Rabbi Eichenstein's son?" Tati asked one day, shortly before I left. "He got divorced, stopped being religious, stopped observing the Shabbos, and he even ate pork, God forbid! Yet he repented, became religious again, and he just got engaged to a nice religious divorcée!"

Oh, Tati, I thought to myself, *why won't you give up on me becoming Hasidic again? There is about as much a chance of me ever becoming Hasidic again as there is of me converting to Christianity.*

"From what I hear," I replied, "he didn't leave because of ideological reasons. People who leave for emotional reasons, or because they found Hasidic Judaism to be too difficult, have a higher chance of coming back. People who leave because of theological and philosophical reasons almost never do."

"Are you telling me that there is no chance at all that you would come back?" Tati asked.

"Pretty much," I said.

I could see the disappointment in his eyes, his face a mix of confusion, sadness, and despair.

"Are you sure about that?" he asked, almost begging. "If you're sure, then what am I even doing?"

In other words, *If there is no chance you will change your mind, why am I still talking to you?*

I didn't have an answer for him, but eventually, he found one of his own.

"I think people who leave the community are sick," he said one day. "If my child had cancer, would I disown him? No!"

So, fine, Tati thought I was sick. At least he still talked to me.

With Mommy, it was different. She was my mother, my nurturer. When we spoke on the phone, she often asked about my religious life. She'd ask how my fast went after a fast day, or if I'd prayed in synagogue on Shabbos. She knew the answers. More likely I'd been hiking with friends on a Saturday, and I hadn't observed a fast day since I'd left. It was hard on both of us, but I knew she was asking because she loved me. More than once, she told me, "I sometimes hope you are right and that God approves of your life. I don't want you to suffer after you pass away." Her religious beliefs were based on a blind faith that set me on edge, but I appreciated her sincerity.

Tati seemed less worried about my soul in the world to come and more concerned with our community's judgment. On Yom Kippur that fall, the holiest day in the Jewish calendar, I went on a camping trip in the woods with friends, bringing with us a very non-kosher menu that included pork. I shared a photograph of it on Facebook, and Tati called me; somehow he had found out about the post, and he was outraged—but not because I'd eaten on Yom Kippur, or even because the food had been *treif.* "Did you have to post pictures about it?" he demanded.

ON THE MORNING of November 11, I arrived at the apartment of my new rabbi and mentor, Rabbi David Ingber. He is the founder and spiritual director of Romemu, a synagogue that celebrates individuality and had become my spiritual home. Romemu is progressive and radically inclusive, a kind of hippie refuge on the Upper West Side that is affiliated with the Jewish Renewal movement.

"He will be here soon," I told him.

Tati was coming. Tati had agreed to meet me at Rabbi David's home, a space were we could talk freely. He had spoken with Rabbi David before, and while he wouldn't usually approve of a rabbi who wasn't Orthodox, he liked Rabbi David, who spoke Tati's Hasidic-style lingo and set him at ease. Rabbi David understood Hasidic Judaism well, which Tati appreciated.

We sat down in the family room and waited. I looked around the room, at the walls lined with bookcases filled with religious Jewish works, including a Talmud and many Hasidic authors, not unlike the ones in Tati's office. I thought about how the two men had so much and so little in common. Both were highly educated and devoted to their communities. But Tati was not a seeker or a skeptic; he had no interest in questioning the edicts of his faith. He knew little about contemporary life, and his worldview was entirely based on his fundamentalist religious beliefs. At the heart of those beliefs were strict definitions of gender, and I knew that any concept of gender or sexuality that was not aligned with his religious and cultural belief system would be sinful in his eyes. Those other ideas had rarely entered the realm of his existence. He was only barely aware that gay people existed, and he had never heard the word "transgender."

He would now.

Soon, Tati rang the bell.

"Shulem Aleichem!" Rabbi David greeted him, using a Yiddish pronunciation of the Hebrew greeting. "Come in and have a seat! Can I get you something?"

"Just water will be fine," Tati said. He wouldn't eat or drink anything other than water in a non-Hasidic home, even one that kept to strict Orthodox kosher standards.

"Hi, Tati," I said with an unusually shy smile.

"Hello," he replied, with the same fatherly smile he'd always had when welcoming me.

I kissed his hand, and he kissed mine back, our standard family greeting.

Then he looked me over and saw that I was not wearing the yarmulke, the obligatory head-covering for boys and men. "Aw, you are not wearing a *kapel*?" Tati noticed.

Before he could say more, his gaze shifted to my ears, or, more exactly, my freshly pierced earlobes, filled with small earrings.

Better keep him focused on the yarmulke for now, I thought.

"I think once we talk you will understand why I am not wearing one," I told Tati.

We all sat down at the table. There was a moment of silence as we all looked at one another. I pulled nervously at my shirt, a tight V-neck with gray and pink stripes. It looked feminine but not immodest; still, Tati came from a culture where men wore only black and white, and pink is a forbidden color, even for women. I could see his gaze settle on my top, then realized it wasn't color he was focusing on. It was the space right below my shoulders.

In such a tight shirt, my nipples were standing out. And not just the nipples. I also had the first signs of breasts.

Just two months previously, I had started hormone replacement therapy, and while I had been feeling a tingling in my chest for weeks, and I had started to see signs of breast growth while in the shower, this was the first time they were visible under a shirt.

Tati looked perplexed.

For a few minutes, Rabbi David and Tati exchanged some pleasantries; they even discussed a Hasidic teaching on that week's reading of the Torah. The text was about the patriarch Isaac, and how he was given a new soul after his father, Abraham, almost sacrificed him.

That seemed like the perfect segue to our conversation.

"Tati, there is something about myself I need to tell you," I started.

And then I explained to him that I was a woman, and that I was going to live as one in the world.

Tati was confused. He looked at me as though what I was saying was impossible, and we did our best to explain.

"You know how the Kabbalists say that people's souls have a gender?" Rabbi David asked.

"Yes . . . "

"Well, they also talk about how souls and bodies can get mixed up, right?" Rabbi David asked.

"Yes, yes—" Tati said. "So?"

"Well, sometimes someone's soul—who they are internally— might not add up to who they are externally. Your child might look like a boy but is actually a girl."

For a while, Rabbi David and Tati did most of the talking, Rabbi David doing his best in Yiddish and Tati struggling with broken English, trying to reach a common ground of comprehension. I sat quietly, suddenly shy and wringing my hands, frustrated that Tati didn't understand and worried about how he would react once he did. Rabbi David sent smiles my way, gestures of kindness and love, keeping the conversation on track when I could not.

Finally, I could see that Tati was beginning to grasp what we were talking about. He still seemed confused, but now his expression seemed to shift into a glimpse of understanding. Impatient, I finally uttered the words I was desperate for him to hear.

"Tati," I said, looking him in the eye. "Tati, I am a girl."

I am a girl. I'd said it.

Tati's eyes flew to the table, avoiding me, fumbling for words. For a moment, there was only silence. Then he spoke.

"But, but—" he stammered. "I don't get it. Men have a higher place in society. Men have better roles in the world. Why would you do that?"

Rabbi David paused for a minute, letting us all take this in. Then he said, "Your child is coming to you and telling you who she truly is. She wants you to see her for *who her soul* is."

We both looked at Tati, but he still wouldn't make eye contact.

More silence.

Fine, I thought, *Tati doesn't believe that is possible. He is going to say that being transgender isn't possible, that trans people don't exist, and he will brush us off.* After all, I had heard far less religious people say such things; I couldn't expect Tati to be any different. This time, however, Tati surprised me.

"Okay, yes," he said. "It is possible that there are people in the world whose souls and bodies are different, and it can be real. But you need a *tzaddik,* a righteous person who has a holy spirit within him, to know that for sure!"

He seemed very sure of his assertion.

"I've seen two therapists and a doctor who all agree with me that I am a girl," I told him. "They are not *tzaddiks,* but they know it's true."

"But do you think that is okay with Judaism?" he lamented.

"I am sitting here with a rabbi," I responded, pointing at Rabbi David, "and you ask me if it's okay with Judaism? My rabbi thinks that it is!"

Tati turned to Rabbi David. "So you agree? You think Judaism accepts this? Do you allow people like this into your synagogue?"

"Definitely!" Rabbi David exclaimed.

"Well," Tati said, looking back at me, "you have to understand that this most likely means I will never be able to talk to you again. Ever."

My heart stopped.

As much as I thought I was prepared for every outcome, nothing could have prepared me to hear my father saying those words.

"What—why?" I asked, tearing up. "Could we talk just on the phone?"

"I don't think so," Tati said, "I will let you know."

I blanked out for the next few minutes. All I could hear was my father telling me we would never speak again. Tati, shunning me. As my heart raced, I was only vaguely aware that Tati and Rabbi David were still talking, and that Tati, who was upset, was also worried about me. He asked fatherly questions about the logistics of my transition, wanting to know if it was okay for my health, and if it was permanent.

The next thing I knew, Tati was standing up, shaking Rabbi David's hand, and then walking to the door.

"Can I talk to Mommy now?" I asked.

"No," Tati said. "I will talk to her. And I will let you know through Rabbi David what I decide about staying in touch."

He opened the door and left.

For the first time in my life, Tati had left me without kissing my hand, or even shaking it. He didn't even say goodbye.

I was shocked.

Rabbi David hugged me and tried to console me, but I was so broken that I couldn't hear his words. I thanked him and wandered into the street, physically exhausted. Then I went home and climbed into bed. But as wrung out as I was, I couldn't sit still. I wanted to say something, I wanted to be heard. I took out my phone and opened up my Facebook account. On my page I posted a quotation from the Book of Prophets, Malachi 2:3:

> He shall turn the heart of the fathers to the children,
> And the heart of the children to their fathers.

And then I took a nap.

"GROWING UP, WE all try to remember our first memories . . . "

After I woke up from my nap that Wednesday late afternoon, I was ready for what came next. I was going to write a letter.

It was a chilly fall night, and I was sitting in my room at Columbia. I lived in a co-op with twenty-eight other students, but the typical noise and bustle outside my door was surprisingly quiet. Or maybe it was noisy and I just couldn't hear it, because I was so deep in my mind and in my memories.

Memories from the past twenty-four years of my life, moments from my childhood and teenage years, were flooding my senses.

It was a coming-out letter.

I was ready to come out as a girl. I was always a girl, now a woman, and I was ready to live in the world that way. The hormones were changing my body to match who I already was on the inside, and I was ready to live a single identity. My truth was clear to me.

But I was also supposed to be a rabbi, a Hasidic man. Everything I had ever been taught told me that I was wrong.

I remembered being four and Mommy calling me a boy. *I am not a boy!* I'd wanted to cry.

I remembered being twelve and sneaking books about sexual relationships that I wasn't supposed to read, looking for a hint of an explanation for what I felt. "How dare you read that?" Tati had screamed.

I remembered being married and wishing I was the bride. Having a child, and wishing I was the mother. "It's a boy," I could hear the doctor saying, emerging from the delivery room. I felt the happiness of that moment all over again. "Are you sure?" I'd asked the doctor when he told me my child was a boy. How could he be sure?

I remembered being told, over and over and over, that I was the continuation of hundreds of years of tradition. That I would become a rabbi, that I would carry on my shoulders the legacy of my holy forefather.

I was writing my letter to tell the world who I really was.

I was a twenty-four-year-old girl who had left her home but wasn't supposed to.

I was a girl who studied at Columbia University even though she had never graduated high school.

I was a girl who had left her fundamentalist religious community, the only one of her parents' thirteen children to do so.

I was a girl who came from a dynasty, a direct descendent of the Baal Shem Tov, the sanctified founder of Hasidic Judaism.

How could I explain all of that in a letter?

I sat back down at my desk. I would have to figure it out because it was time. I clicked open the letter and began to type.

I wrote about the day when I was twenty and used the Internet for the first time. That was the day I learned that my experience had a name, *gender dysphoria*.

I wrote about growing up in a community that shunned outside media, and how without access to movies and TV shows, music, and magazines, I didn't know that other transgender people existed.

I wrote about how I had dreamed of a magical place that would turn me into a girl.

I wrote about how I had prayed every night, *Please, Holy One, let me wake up as a girl.*

I wrote and wrote until I was done. I signed the bottom, "Full of love, Abby (Srully Abe) Stein." And I sent it.

I sent it to my housemates, my classmates, my friends. I posted it to my blog, too, a small site I'd named The Second Transition, a place where I uploaded my observations and experiences for the handful of people who visited my site.

I logged into all my social media accounts and changed my name to Abby Stein. I changed my profile picture on Facebook to a photo of me with concealer and blush, and I posted a link to my blog post.

When that was done, I went to the bathroom, brushed my teeth, applied face moisturizer, and put on a pink floral shirt I had bought a few weeks before.

Then I went to bed, and it was the best I'd slept in years.

I WOKE UP the next morning to the sound of my phone blowing up.

There were messages—hundreds of them! Facebook, my blog, my email account, all were pinging me with notifications and new messages and friend requests, many from people I'd never heard of. In my email was a request for an interview from *The Yiddish Forward* and another one from the *New York Post*. It was beautiful!

So many people had posted comments. "Congratulations!" they wrote. And "I'm so happy for you!" Friends and strangers alike were encouraging me in ways I'd never imagined! Some wrote that I was brave, others called me inspiring, and many wished me well on my journey. Every note offered kindness and encouragement. Some girlfriends offered to take me shopping for new clothes. Another sent me a gift card to Sephora. A transgender woman wanted to know how I was doing with my hormones. A Columbia professor asked if I needed any support at school while going through my transition.

Yes, Tati said that he and Mommy might never speak to me again. Yes, of my twelve siblings, ten stopped speaking to me, and so had most of my extended family. But I was not alone. After twenty-four years of secrecy, fear, and shame, the outpouring of love was overwhelming.

FOR A LONG time, my conversation with Tati hung over my head. It hadn't ended the way I'd hoped; the sight of him walking away from me played over in my head for days. I found solace in friends, and they filled my new life with a kind of acceptance I'd never experienced before. Of course, there were the celebratory posts and emails that continued to cover my social media walls and fill my inbox, but there were also the private, intimate friendships that showed me that I, Abby Stein, would never be alone.

When I first started hormone replacement therapy, I'd wondered what it would be like to tell the world. What would people say? How would they react? What questions would they ask? I hadn't been ready to come out publicly quite yet, but I also couldn't keep my news entirely to myself. So I'd decided to tell a friend. On Saturday afternoon, the day after I'd started taking hormone treatments, I invited my friend Talia to my room. I chose Talia not only because she was a close friend, but because she'd also grown up Orthodox. She had become an outspoken ally for the LGBTQ+ community.

In my room, Talia sat down on the couch, and I sat down on my chair. I shook with anxiety, unsure where to begin. Finally I picked up the small bottle of Estradiol, a form of estrogen pills, and handed them to Talia.

"Do you know what this is?" I asked.

"No," Talia said. She looked worried for me.

"Well, it's estrogen," I said. "You know, the female hormone."

Her face relaxed in relief that I wasn't sick, and then brightened with a wide smile. "So, you are . . . ?"

She looked at me, waiting for me to say it.

"Yes. I am a girl. I am trans, and I just started to transition." I returned her gaze expectantly. I'd said it!

"That is amazing!" Talia said. Her happiness for me lifted a weight from my chest, and I returned her smile, thrilled. We chatted easily after that—she asked me questions about my transition, and I filled her in.

"So," she said with a wink, "when are we having a girls' night out?"

I felt the love.

SINCE THEN, I have had the privilege and honor to engage with hundreds of thousands of people from all over the world, and the support I've been given has not stopped growing. Yes, I've seen the uglier side of human nature. I've received transphobic screeds, anti-Semitic attacks, and messages of hate from people who loathe me even more for being both. I've been threatened, I've been wished dead. But even the loudest voices of hate have been just a dark dot in a sea of light, the light of acceptance, tolerance, and celebration. I've seen more kindness than I ever expected in a lifetime, and I've learned more about the world, and identity, and faith, in these past few years than I could have ever imagined.

Today I live fully as a woman, and I get to share my story often. But I've only told it in parts and in pieces, and it's the whole of my story that has led me to who I am now.

That story is still happening. This is only the beginning.

To be continued!

ACKNOWLEDGMENTS

This book, like my life and my life story, would not have been the same without the amazing people—the organizations, professionals, and friends—who have come into my life. I will forever be grateful to so many who continue to make my life, personally and communally, better and better every day. While I can't mention everyone, as the Mishna says, "It is not on you to complete all the work there is; however, you are still not free to ignore it." So if I can't mention everyone, I will include as many as I can.

First and foremost, thank you to everyone who made this book possible:

Thank you to my agent, Kate Johnson, without whom I would not have written this book anytime soon, and who pushed me, in the most graceful way possible, to stick to my deadlines (which I did, roughly). She has also been responsible for all my speaking events and media engagements over the past three years, and thanks to her work, I have delivered hundreds of speeches around the globe. Thank you also to her whole team at MacKenzie Wolf Literary Agency.

Thank you to my editor, Laura Mazer, who guided me throughout the entire process of writing and revising this book.

From the moment of our first phone call to the minute I am writing these words today, she believed in me always, even in the hardest times, even when I myself doubted if I would be able to write this book.

Thank you to my publicist, Sharon Kunz, with her spot-on instincts for everything related to sharing this book with the world. And of course, to the team of copyeditors, proofreaders, designers, publishing executives, and beyond at Seal Press, and its parent company, Hachette Book Group.

Beyond the book, the biggest gratitude in my life for the past seven-plus years undoubtedly goes to Footsteps, the life-saving organization that is helping those who wish to leave the Ultra-Orthodox Jewish world. Without Footsteps' support, I would not have experienced any of my successes, and I would not be who I am today.

I want to thank many special people at Footsteps, but here are a few:

Thank you to Lani Santo, the executive director and the only staff member who has been with Footsteps since the day I joined. From the minute we met, she believed in me, encouraged me, and gave me numerous opportunities, including appearing in Footsteps' tenth-anniversary gala video (my first public appearance outside of the Hasidic world). She has given me constant advice and been a nonstop cheerleader. On an organizational level, I have watched Lani take Footsteps from a small organization of three staff members, 300 or so members, and a small budget to a group with close to twenty staff members, more than 1,500 members, and a budget in the millions.

To Michael Jenkins, the social worker at Footsteps when I joined, and the first person in my life I ever spoke to who truly understood me. To Alix Newpol, who showed me so much of what a life outside of the Hasidic community can look like. Jesse Pietroniro, one of Footsteps' former social workers, who was one of the first people I came out to in the summer of 2015, and who guided me through the first few crucial months of my physical transition. To Chavie Weissberger, Chani Getter, Tsivia Finman, and the other Footsteps staff who grew up Ultra-Orthodox, and who constantly give back to the community—all have offered me friendship in so many ways.

To my close cousins who were also Footsteps members, Chaim Meisels, Luzer Twersky, and those in the closet; to Nataly, Mindle Shavy, Penny, Goldy, Naftuli, Shulem, Leah, Shaindy, Gene and Mary, Sarah, and so many other Footsteps members who became my personal friends, from best friends to acquaintances. The Footsteps community, and every individual within it, offers the best answer to the question, "Is it is possible to live a full life after leaving fundamentalism?" Footsteps says, wholeheartedly, yes.

After leaving the Hasidic community, I went through a period when I felt that Judaism no longer had anything to offer me. Romemu, founded and led by Rabbi David Ingber, has shown me that I can enjoy the aspects I like, and let go of the weight I don't. The Romemu community unconditionally loves, supports, and celebrates me, and has shown me an elevated Jewish path to Shabbat, holidays, and lifecycles that is radically inclusive. As readers will learn in the epilogue of this book, Romemu has also been instrumental in supporting me in my transition and giving me space to celebrate my identity. Rabbi David Ingber offered his help when I came out to my father, and he was there to support me in the aftermath, when I experienced something no one should have to: family rejection. Rabbi Jessica Kate Meyer was the first person I came out to at Romemu, months before I came out publicly, and her love showed me what a Jewish world of acceptance looks like. Rabbi Mira Rivera and Hazzan Basya Schechter, along with others at Romemu, helped me create my beautiful Coming Out/Naming/Bat Mitzvah celebration in May 2016.

Thank you to those at Columbia University:

I am grateful to the late School of General Studies dean, Peter Awn—may his memory be a blessing—who pushed me to apply and showed a keen interest not only in my academics but also in my personal life. With his constant smile and witty remarks, he knew what to say at every moment, drawing on his own experience with religious fundamentalism and LGBTQ life.

To my advisers—Sara, RJ, and the rest of the deans of students—who supported me from the beginning, as I was navigating a modern classroom for the first time in my life. To Community Impact at Columbia University, the volunteer-run group where I took the first college classes in my life, and who offered me a free taste of Columbia before I applied.

To so many professors who went above and beyond, taking into account my personal struggles as they influenced my learning. The list is long, but they know who they are.

To GS Alliance, the LGBTQ student group at the School of General Studies at Columbia; the Columbia Queer Alliance, the university-wide LGBTQ student group; GendeRevolution, Columbia's trans student support group; and the Columbia Atheist Agnostic Student Society. The General Studies student body, as well as many other student groups, made me feel at home at Columbia before, during, and after my transition.

ACKNOWLEDGMENTS

Above all, I am forever grateful to my second home at Columbia: Columbia Barnard Hillel. From the first moment I walked through the doors of the Kraft Center, I have felt I had a home—I have celebrated Shabbat meals, holidays, Passover seders, and more at Columbia Hillel. The list of people to thank on the staff is long, but I will mention three here: Rabbi Yonah Hain, who became not just a teacher but a friend and, dare I say, a colleague; executive director Brian Cohn, who—in addition to his phenomenal leadership transforming Columbia Barnard Hillel into one of the biggest Jewish student groups on any college campus—has supported me constantly; and last but by far not least, Rabbi Megan GoldMarche, who was the first person I came out to as I began my transition journey.

There are so many students I would love to thank, but I know if I start, I will never finish. I'll mention just one, who you will read about in the epilogue: Talia Lakritz, who was the first friend I came out to, and who has been a friend, mentor, and vocal supporter. I also want to mention my amazing housemates at the Bayit, the Columbia Jewish food co-op where I lived for two years, and my group of twelve close friends at the School of General Studies—you know who you are!

From the most personal parts of my life, I want to thank my family. I know many of them will never read these words, and that my feelings of love are not fully reciprocated. However, as the dedication page of the book indicates, "Mighty waters cannot quench love."

Thank you to Mommy and Tati, who gave me life and showed me what a loving family could look like. I love you both forever and ever, even from afar. To my twelve siblings: Hanna Zissel, Ruchel'a, Esther Gitti, Faigy, Hindi, Hershy, Efroim, Zalmen

Leib, Baruch, Suri, Miriam, and Tzirel, and all of their children. Regardless of how you might feel about me today, I learned so much from all of you and I love you all. I know you don't want me to mention your names, but to the two siblings who still talk to me: you are a symbol of real love and real family. They are no words to express how much I love you both, and how grateful I am.

To the dozen or so cousins who continue to stay in touch with me: Thank you for showing me that I do still have real family. Zaide and Bobbe Meisels: I like to think that if you were alive, you would accept me. Zaide would tell me his amazing stories from "back home" in Europe, the heroism of his life during the Holocaust, and his life with his teachers in pre-State Jerusalem. Bobbe's smile, encouraging words, and amazing rugelach recipe are all with me, and they will be forever. My you both rest in peace.

Zaide and Bobbe Stein: you were truly my second set of parents. The weekends and holidays I spent in your house as a teenager, the meaningful songs, the delicious food, and the loving atmosphere all guide me to this day. I hope, I wish, that one day, soon, I will see you again.

Thank you to the three women in my life who have shown me that love and intimacy is possible after leaving fundamentalism, and after transitioning.

One final thank you:

The love of my life, my child, Duvid'l. Thank you for showing me how much love a person can have for another; for being the ray of light in my darkest days; for being the most essential part of my life. Forever and ever, you are with me and I am with you.

Abby Stein is a Jewish educator, speaker, and trans activist. Born and raised in a Hasidic family of rabbinic descent, she attended yeshiva and completed a rabbinical degree in 2011. In 2012, Stein left the Hasidic enclave to explore a self-determined life, and in 2015 she came out as a woman of trans experience. Since coming out, she has worked to raise awareness and support others with similar experiences. Her story has been covered in *Vogue*, the *New York Times*, the *New York Post*, *New York* magazine, *Jewish Daily Forward*, the *Daily Mail*, *InStyle*, and more, and she has made live appearances on Fox News, CNN, i24 News, Studio 10, ABC Australia, and more. Stein regularly lectures and leads text studies for Jewish and LGBTQ+ groups, and she served on the national steering committee for the Women's March. Preet Bharara selected her in his CAFE 100 list of change-makers in 2018, and in 2016 she was recognized by the *Jewish Week* in its annual "36 Under 36" profile of emerging young Jewish leaders. In 2018, she received the Pride Award from Brooklyn's borough president, Eric Adams, for her "bravery and advocacy work around trans issues in the ultra-Orthodox community." She studied at Columbia University focusing on gender studies and political science. Her blog, The Second Transition, has garnered hundreds of thousands of views and is available at www.abbychavastein.com.